The HUMAN CONNECTION

How People Change People

Martin Bolt & David G. Myers

InterVarsity Press
Downers Grove
Illinois 60515

InterVarsity Press is the book-publishing division of Inter-Varsity Christian Fellowship, a student movement active on campus at hundreds of universities, colleges and schools of nursing. For information about local and regional activities, write IVCF, 233 Langdon St., Madison, WI 53703.

Distributed in Canada through InterVarsity Press, 860 Denison St., Unit 3, Markham, Ontario L3R 4H1, Canada.

Cover photograph: David Singer

ISBN 0-87784-913-7

Printed in the United States of America

Library of Congress Cataloging in Publication Data
Bolt, Martin, 1944-
    The human connection.

    Includes bibliographical references.
    1. Christian life–1960-   –Addresses, essays,
lectures. 2. Social psychology–Addresses, essays,
lectures. I. Myers, David G. II. Title.
BV4501.2.B6182   1984   302   83-20420
ISBN 0-87784-913-7

17	16	15	14	13	12	11	10	9	8	7	6	5	4	3	2	1
98	97	96	95	94	93	92	91	90	89	88	87	86	85	84		

Acknowledgments

With appreciation we acknowledge our collaborators who worked with us in preparing several essays in this book. To John Shaughnessy, Thomas Ludwig, John Brink, and Steven Hoogerwerf go our sincere thanks. We are indebted to many friends and colleagues who read these essays in earlier form and offered constructive suggestions and criticisms. Special thanks are also due Jean Brasser and Kathy Adamski for their predictably excellent typing and word-processing skills in the final preparation of the manuscript.

As is true in most cooperative efforts of this type, the primary responsibility for the various chapters was divided between us. The authors primarily responsible for each chapter are named in the table of contents. Earlier versions of certain essays have appeared elsewhere:

Chapter 2: *Christianity Today* (18 November 1980).

Chapter 3: C. Ellison, ed., *Your Better Self* (Harper and Row, 1983); *Psychology Today* (August 1979); *Christian Century* (1 December 1982).

Chapter 4: D. G. Myers, *The Inflated Self* (Seabury, 1980); D. G. Myers, *Social Psychology* (McGraw-Hill, 1983).

Chapter 5: *Science Digest* (August 1981); *Christianity Today* (15 July 1983).

Chapter 6: *Church Herald* (21 March 1980); *Christian Ministry* (January 1981); *Military Chaplain's Review* (Summer 1981).

Chapter 9: *The Banner* (19 and 26 September 1975); *CAPS Bulletin*, vol. 7, no. 2 (1981).

Chapter 10: *Saturday Review* (28 October 1978); *Christian Century* (30 May 1979).

Chapter 13: *The Banner* (28 December 1979).

1
A Social World

THE COLLEGE BOARD recently invited the million high-school seniors taking its aptitude test to indicate "how you feel you compare with other people your own age in certain areas of ability." Sixty per cent reported themselves as better than average in "athletic ability." In "leadership ability" 70 per cent rated themselves as above average, 2 per cent as below average. In "ability to get along with others," less than 1 per cent of the 829,000 students who responded rated themselves as below average, 60 per cent rated themselves in the top 10 per cent, and 25 per cent saw themselves among the top 1 per cent.

Judging from the students' responses, America's high-school seniors are hardly plagued with inferiority feelings. Why then do so many psychologists and preachers lament our low self-esteem? How do we really feel about ourselves—

and what should we as Christians be doing about self-image?

Think back to last Sunday morning's sermon. Can you recall the major points or the theme? Psychologist Thomas Crawford and his associates went to the homes of people from twelve churches shortly before and after they heard a sermon opposing racial injustice. When asked during the second interview whether they had heard or read anything about racial prejudice or discrimination since the previous interview, only 10 per cent spontaneously recalled the sermon. When the remaining 90 per cent were asked directly whether their preacher "talked about prejudice or discrimination in the last couple of weeks," more than 30 per cent denied hearing such a sermon.

Is this typical of the impact of sermons? How might each of us who must teach, speak or write do so with more effect than these preachers? And what can we do to receive maximum benefit from what we hear and read?

Now imagine that you and some others have come to participate in a psychological study of emotional cues. By what appears to be random choice, one of the participants, actually an accomplice of the experimenter, is selected to perform a memory task. She is to receive painful shocks for any error made while you and the other participants note her emotional response. After watching her grimace in response to a number of seemingly painful shocks, you are asked to evaluate her. How will you respond? With compassion and sympathy? Probably not. When observers are powerless to alter a victim's fate, they tend to reject and devalue her—as if such a bad thing couldn't happen to a good person.

This research finding tells a lot about how we view victims of oppression. Do we acknowledge that bad things *can* happen to good people? Or do we just mirror the thoughts of Job's friends, believing that people get what they deserve?

These three examples, taken from forthcoming chapters, illustrate the broad concerns of social psychology. How we think about ourselves and others (the ratings of the high-school seniors), influence one another (the sermons) and relate to each other (the evaluations of the punished woman) are what the discipline is all about. Certainly these are not new concerns. Conformity and independence, love and hate, persuasion and peacemaking all form the fabric of everyday life. They are familiar and visible—in poetry, philosophy and theology, on the streets and in our churches.

While the questions social psychologists ask are hardly new, their approach is unique. They look for answers through careful observation and experimentation. This systematic, scientific approach to human social behavior is a young discipline. It is, in fact, a twentieth-century phenomenon. And while much mystery remains, important insights into human relationships are already emerging.

In this book we hope to communicate some of the fascination of the search, to present some of the more provocative findings and to consider the implications of these findings for Christian belief and everyday life. These issues, and therefore this book, are for all Christians who wrestle with the task of living obediently and who want to influence others to make Jesus Christ the Lord of their lives.

Believing, Influencing, Relating: A Three-Part Study
Part I of our book explores recent research on how and what people believe. Social psychologists have learned some surprising things concerning the relationship of faith and works. Studies have also been done on how we think about ourselves. What kinds of complexes do we really suffer from? The findings provide a fresh retelling of ancient biblical wisdom. We will also examine some disturbing new experiments which suggest how and why people come to form false beliefs.

A fundamental aspect of our social nature is how we influence and are influenced by our fellow human beings. In Part II we explore the nature and extent of this social influence. For example, what kinds of messages are most memorable and persuasive? Do rewards persuade too? We will look not only at how persuasive rewards are, but how much actual constructive change they effect. The implications for Christian parenting and Christian education are telling. The scriptural command "Be not conformed . . ." will assume new meaning as we look at how readily social forces shape our behavior and our beliefs. We will see how "groupthink" creeps into the local church and suggest how we can think together as Christians without falling into such traps.

Our social relationships provide the basis for our deepest satisfactions as well as our most difficult challenges. Part III will explore some of the central themes that run through our relationships with one another. We will examine comparisons people make with each other and the strange phenomenon of "poortalk" that often results. Analyzing the research done on human attraction, we'll see what makes us naturally move toward certain people—and compare that tendency with Christ's command to love. When will we offer aid to those in need? Studies on altruism show how much our willingness to help is influenced by situational factors. Our willingness may be further complicated by our need to believe in a just world. Recent findings indicate that the "justice motive" may lead to more than Christian compassion. We conclude Part III with some of the key principles that are foundational for all Christian peacemaking.

"It is not good that the man should be alone" (Gen 2:18 RSV). And thus God created us interdependent, not self-sufficient; social, not isolated. Join with us now as we explore some of psychology's recent findings regarding our social nature and probe their significance for Christian faith and practice.

Part I
Believing

BELIEF IS CENTRAL in the Christian life. Paul tells us we are saved by grace through faith. Jesus, during the storm on the Sea of Galilee, asked his fearful disciples why they had so little faith. How do we come to believe what we believe? How can we be sure that what we believe is true?

Part I takes up these and related issues. Chapter two considers how faith and obedience relate. Popular wisdom stresses the impact of our attitudes on our actions. In the church, teaching and preaching follow this thinking by aiming to change the heart, assuming obedience will follow. This chapter examines the less commonsensical idea that behavior determines beliefs.

Among our most central beliefs are those we hold about ourselves. The notion that most of us suffer from unrealistically low self-esteem has become widely accepted within the Christian community. Presumably we need to develop a healthier, more positive self-image. Chapter three looks at the other side of the coin. Do most people actually have a "self-serving bias"? Is pride the more common error? Does an inflated self-perception alienate us from God and lead us to disdain one another? How can recognizing our pride as sin draw us to Christ and to a positive self-regard rooted in his grace?

Objectivity—or the lack of it—can also drive a wedge between people. While in the past social psychologists have viewed us as rational animals, recently their attention has shifted to errors in our thinking that may prejudice our judgments of others. Chapter four examines the way people form and sustain false beliefs reinforces St. Paul's contention that human wisdom is not nearly so wise as God's foolishness.

Chapter five asks, Why do people believe in paranormal events and powers in the face of great evidence against their existence? The point is not that psychic phenomena do not exist but that, whether they do or not, illusory thinking almost guarantees that people will invent such beliefs. At issue is our whole understanding of ourselves and others: Do we have paranormal abilities? Or are we finite creatures of the one who declares "I am God, and there is none like me"?

2
Behavior
and
Belief

PEOPLE GENERALLY ASSUME that our beliefs and attitudes determine our actions. So if we want to change the way people act, their hearts and minds had better be changed. This assumption lies behind most of our teaching, preaching, counseling and child rearing. But if social psychology has taught us anything during the last twenty years it is that the reverse is equally true: we are as likely to act ourselves into a way of thinking as to think ourselves into action.

Let's take a peek at this action-attitude research, see how it squares with the biblical understanding of faith and action, and then consider practical implications for church life and Christian nurture.

Action and Attitude
Social psychologists agree that attitudes and actions have a

Action

Attitude

Figure 1.   Interaction of action and attitude.

reciprocal relationship, each feeding on the other (figure 1). In fact, the effect of our attitudes on our actions seems not so great as most people suppose.[1] The attitudes people express toward the church, for example, are only moderately related to their church attendance on any given Sunday. The fact is, any particular action, such as going or not going to church on June 1, is the product of many influences, not just one's attitude toward the church. So it is not surprising that attempts to change people's behavior by changing their attitudes often produce only modest results. Habits like smoking, television watching and bad driving practices are not affected much by persuasive appeals.[2]

Although attitudes determine our behavior less than commonly supposed, the complementary proposition—that behavior determines attitude—turns out to be far more true than most people think. We are as likely to believe in what we have stood up for as to stand up for what we believe. Many streams of evidence converge to establish this principle. Consider two:

The foot-in-the-door phenomenon.   A number of experiments indicate that if you want people to do a big favor for you, it's wise to get them to do a small favor first. In the best-known demonstration of this, Jonathan Freedman and Scott Fraser wanted California housewives to place a large, ugly "Drive Carefully" sign on their front lawns. Tests showed that they were more likely to do this if they had first been asked to do the smaller favor of signing a safe-driving petition.[3]

In this situation, as in countless other experiments demonstrating the effect of action on attitude, the behavior (signing the petition) was a chosen, public act. Time and again,

social psychologists have found that when people bind
themselves to public behavior *and* perceive this as their own
doing, they come to believe more strongly in their action.
Also, the effect on the housewives' attitudes was evident
in their subsequent willingness to perform an even more
substantial action, demonstrating the reciprocal influence
of action and attitude.

Sometimes action and attitude feed one another in a spiraling escalation. In his well-known experiments, Stanley Milgram induced adult men to deliver supposedly traumatizing
electric shocks to an innocent victim in an adjacent room.[4]
People were commanded to deliver the shock (said to be
punishment for wrong answers on a learning task) in steps
gradually increasing from 15 to 450 volts. The troubling
result—that 65 per cent of the participants complied right
up to 450 volts even while the supposed victim screamed
his protests—seems partly due to an effective use of the foot-
in-the-door principle. Their first act was trivial (15 volts),
and the next (30 volts) was not noticeably more severe. By
the time the supposed victim first indicated mild discomfort
the participant had already bound himself to the situation
on several occasions, and the next act was, again, not noticeably more severe. External behavior and internal disposition
can amplify one another, especially when social pressures
induce actions that are increasingly extreme. And so it is that
ordinary people can become unwitting agents of evil.

Effects of moral and immoral acts.   All this suggests the
more general possibility that acting in violation of one's
moral standards may set in motion a process of self-justification which leads ultimately to sincere belief in the act. Experiments bear this out. People induced to give witness to
something about which they have doubts will generally
begin to believe their "little lies," at least if they felt some
sense of choice in the matter. Saying is believing. Likewise,
harming an innocent victim—by muttering a cutting comment or delivering shocks—typically leads aggressors to

disparage their victims, especially if the aggressors are coaxed rather than coerced into doing so.[5] Wartime provides the most tragic real-life parallel to these laboratory findings: here we know too well how immoral acts corrode the moral sensitivity of the actors.

Fortunately, the principle cuts in the other direction as well. Moral action has positive effects on the actor. Experiments demonstrate that when children are induced to resist temptation, they tend to internalize their conscientious behavior, especially if the deterrent is mild enough to leave them with a sense of choice.[6] Moreover, children who are actively engaged in enforcing rules or in teaching moral norms to younger children subsequently follow the moral code better than children who are not given the opportunity to be teachers or enforcers.[7] Generalizing the principle, it would seem that one antidote for the corrupting effects of evil action is repentant action. Evil acts shape the self, but moral acts do so as well.

These few examples illustrate why the attitudes-follow-behavior principle has become an accepted theory in contemporary social psychology. Since the phenomenon is more clearly established than its explanation, social psychologists have been busy playing detective, trying to track down clues that would reveal *why* action affects attitude. One explanation suggests that we are motivated to justify our actions as a way of relieving the discomfort we feel when our behavior differs noticeably from our prior attitude. An alternative explanation is that when our attitudes are weak or ambiguous, we observe our actions and then infer what attitudes we must have, given how we have acted. What we say and do can sometimes be quite self-revealing! Neither of these views necessarily implies that the effect of action is a mindless irrational process. Our thinking is stimulated by our action. The reasons we develop to explain our actions can be real and intellectually defensible. As one student explained, "It wasn't until I tried to verbalize my beliefs that found I was really able to understand them."

Regardless of what explanation is best, we can find a practical moral for us all: each time we act, we strengthen the idea behind what we have done. We increase our inclination to act in the same way again. If we want to change ourselves in some important way, we had better not depend exclusively on introspection and intellectual insight. Sometimes we need to get up and do something—begin writing that paper, make those phone calls, go see that person—even if we do not feel like moving. If Moses, Jonah and others had waited until they felt like doing what God was calling them to do, their missions would never have been accomplished. (Indeed, if not acted on, ideas often begin to fade until recharged by new action.) Fortunately, we often discover that once we have written the first paragraph or made the first call, our commitment and enthusiasm for what we are doing begins to take hold of us and drive us forward with its own momentum.

Action and Faith

The social psychological evidence that action and attitude generate one another in an endless chain—like chicken and egg—affirms and enlivens the biblical understanding of action and faith. Depending on where we break into this spiraling chain, we will see how faith can be a source of action or how it can be a consequence of action. Both perspectives are correct, since action and faith, like action and attitude, feed one another.

Christian thinking has usually emphasized faith as the source of action, just as conventional wisdom has insisted that our attitudes determine our behavior. Faith, we believe, is the beginning rather than the end of religious development. For example, the experience of being "called" demonstrates how faith can precede action in the lives of the faithful. Elijah is overwhelmed by the Holy as he huddles in a cave. Paul is touched by the Almighty on the Damascus

Road. Ezekiel, Isaiah, Jeremiah and Amos are likewise invaded by the Word, which then explodes in their active response to the call. In each case, an encounter with God provoked a new state of consciousness which was then acted on.

This dynamic potential of faith is already a central tenet of evangelical thought. For the sake of balance, we should also appreciate the complementary proposition: Faith is a consequence of action. Throughout the Old and New Testaments we are told that full knowledge of God comes through actively *doing* the Word. Faith is nurtured by obedience.

Reinhold Niebuhr and others have called attention to the contrast in assumptions between biblical thought and the Platonic thought that permeates our Western culture today. Plato presumed that we come to know truth by reason and quiet reflection. This view, translated into Christian terms, equates faith with cerebral activity—orthodox doctrinal propositions, for example.

The contrasting biblical view assumes that reality is known through obedient commitment. As O. A. Piper has written in the *Interpreter's Dictionary of the Bible*, "This feature, more than any other, brings out the wide gulf which separates the Hebraic from the Greek view of knowledge. In the latter, knowledge itself is purely theoretical ... whereas in the Old Testament the person who does not act in accordance with what God has done or plans to do has but a fragmentary knowledge."[8] For example, the Hebrew word for *know* is generally used as a verb, something you do. To know love, we must not only know about love but we must act lovingly. Likewise, to *hear* the word of God means not only to listen but also to obey.

We read in the New Testament that by loving action a person knows God, for "he who does what is true comes to the light" (Jn 3:21 RSV). Jesus declared that whoever would do the will of God would know God, that he would come and dwell within those who heed what he said, and that we would find ourselves not by passive contemplation but by losing ourselves as we take up the cross. The wise man, the one who built his house on rock, differed from the foolish man in that he acted on God's Word. Merely saying "Lord, Lord" does not qualify us as disciples; discipleship means doing the will of the Father. Over and over again, the Bible teaches that gospel power can only be known by living it.

Our theological understanding of faith is built on this biblical view of knowledge. Faith grows as we act on what little faith we have. Just as experimental subjects become more deeply committed to something for which they have suffered and witnessed, so also do we grow in faith as we act it out. Faith "is born of obedience," said John Calvin. "The proof of Christianity really consists in 'following,' " declared Søren Kierkegaard. Karl Barth agreed: "Only the doer of the Word is its real hearer."

C. S. Lewis captured this dynamic of faith in his Chronicles of Narnia. The great lion Aslan has returned to Narnia to redeem his captive creatures. Lucy, a young girl with a trusting, childlike faith in Aslan, catches a glimpse of him and eventually convinces the others in her party to start walking toward where she sees him. As Lucy follows Aslan, she comes to see him more clearly. The others, skeptical and grumbling at first, follow despite their doubts. Only as they follow do they begin to see what was formerly invisible to them—first a fleeting hint of the lion, then his shadow, until finally, after many steps, they see him face to face. As Dietrich Bonhoeffer concluded in The Cost of Discipleship, "Only he who believes is obedient, and only he who is obedient believes. . . . You can only know and think about it by actually doing it."9

Christians will surely want to understand and communicate their faith as rationally defensible. Yet when Jesus counseled that the kingdom of God belongs to those who come like a child, he reminded us that codified intellectual understanding need not precede faith. Jesus called people to follow him, not just to believe in a creed. Peter dropped his nets, leaving all behind, when Jesus called him. Only much later did he verbalize his conviction with the declaration: "You are the Christ." Although we must remember that justification is the gift of God—Peter does not achieve his own conversion—the meaning of faith is nevertheless learned through obedient action.

Implications for Church Life and Christian Nurture

How can we apply these principles to, say, leading a church, to planning worship, and to nurturing personal faith? First, a top priority for churches must be to make their members active participants, not mere spectators. Many dynamic religious movements today, ranging from sects like the Jehovah's Witnesses, Mormons and the Unification Church to charismatics and discipleship-centered communities, share an insistence that all on board be members of the crew. That is easier said than done, but it does provide a criterion by which to evaluate procedures for admitting and maintaining members. As a local church makes decisions and administers its program, it should constantly be asking, Will this activate our people and make priests of our believers? If research on persuasion is any indication, this will best be accomplished by direct, personal calls to committed action, not merely by mass appeals and announcements.

In worship, too, people should be engaged as active participants, not as mere spectators of religious theater. Research indicates that passively received spoken words have surprisingly little impact on listeners. Changes in attitude resulting from spoken persuasion are less likely to endure and influence subsequent behavior than attitude changes emerging from active experience.[10] What's needed is to have listeners rehearse and act on what they hear. If the church is liturgical, then the congregation needs to participate actively in the ritual. The public act of choosing to get out of one's seat and kneel publicly before the congregation in taking Communion is but one example. Going forward to demonstrate repentance or commitment, giving a public testimony or participating in believers' baptism are others. When the people sing responses, write their own confessions, contribute prayer, read Scripture responsively, take notes on the sermon, utter exclamations, bring their offerings forward, pass the peace, make the sign of the cross, or sit, stand and kneel—acts that viewers of the electronic church do not perform—they are making their worship their own.

The principle has its limits, of course. We can become so preoccupied with doing things that we no longer have time to quietly receive God's Word of grace and direction for our lives. Like the Pharisees, we can substitute our deeds for God's act, or think that any kind of action will do. To say that action nurtures growth in faith is not to tell the whole story of faith. But it does tell part of the story.

The action-attitude principle can also help us with Christian education and Christian nurture. Since researchers have found that the attitudes we form by experience are most likely to affect our actions, we might consider new methods of encouraging faith. For example, few Christian families appreciate and reap the benefits of family worship. Old Testament family practices helped people remember the mighty acts of God. When today's Jewish family celebrates the Passover by eating special foods, reading prayers and singing psalms, all of which symbolize their historical experience, they are helped to renew the roots of deep convictions and feelings. As Tevye exclaimed in *Fiddler on the Roof,* "Because of our traditions every one of us knows who he is and what God expects him to do. . . . Without our traditions our lives would be as shaky as a fiddler on the roof." Among Christians, family celebrations are becoming more common during Advent. With a boost from the church, home-based activity could be extended to celebrate all the great themes of the church year.

Although church and family ritual may sometimes degenerate into a superficial religious exercise, few of us appreciate the extent to which the natural ritual of our own personal histories has shaped who we are. Many of the things we did without question in childhood have long since become an enduring part of our self-identities. Indeed, because we have internalized our own rituals, we find it difficult to recognize them as rituals; but it is easy to recognize other people's rituals.

The overarching objective on which all these points converge is this: we want to create opportunities for people to enact their convictions, thereby confirming and strengthening their Christian identity. Biblical and psychological perspectives link arms in reminding us that faith is like love. If we hoard it, it will shrivel. If we use it, exercise it and express it, we will have it more abundantly.

3
The Inflated Self: A New Look at Pride

Poised somewhere between sinful vanity and self-destructive submissiveness is a golden mean of self-esteem appropriate to the human condition.
Stanford Lyman

THERE IS NO DOUBT about it. High self-esteem pays dividends. Those with a positive self-image are happier, freer of ulcers and insomnia, less prone to drug and alcohol addictions. Researchers have also found that people whose ego is temporarily deflated—say, by being told that they did miserably on an intelligence test—are more likely to disparage other people or even express heightened racial prejudice. More generally, people who are negative about themselves tend to be negative about others. Low self-esteem can feed contemptuous attitudes.

What people believe about themselves can have a profound impact on their lives. Those who believe they can control their own destiny—who have what researchers in more than a thousand studies have called "internal locus of control"—achieve more, make more money and are less vulnerable to being manipulated.[1] Believe that things are beyond your control, and they probably will be. Believe that you can do it, and maybe you will.

Knowing this may encourage us not to resign ourselves to bad situations but to persist despite initial failures, to strive without being derailed by self-doubts. But as Pascal taught, no single truth is ever sufficient because the world is not simple. Any truth separated from its complementary truth is a half-truth. That high self-esteem and positive thinking pay dividends is true. But in heralding this truth let us not forget another more disturbing truth—the truth about the pervasiveness and the pitfalls of pride. To remind us of this neglected second truth, consider social psychology's new look at pride.

The Self-serving Bias

It is popularly believed that most of us suffer the "I'm not OK—You're OK" type of low self-esteem. As Groucho Marx put it, "I'd never join any club that would accept a person like me." Carl Rogers described this low self-image problem when he objected to Reinhold Niebuhr's idea that original sin is self-love, pretention, pride. No, no, replied Rogers, Niebuhr had it backwards. People's problems arise because "they despise themselves, regard themselves as worthless and unlovable."

The issue between Niebuhr and Rogers is very much alive today. And what an intriguing irony it is that so many Christian writers are now echoing Rogers and the other prophets of humanistic psychology at the very time that research psychologists are amassing new data concerning the pervasiveness of pride. Indeed, the orthodox theologians, not the humanistic psychologists, seem closer to the truth. As writer William Saroyan put it, "Every man is a good man in a bad world—as he himself knows."

Researchers are debating the reasons for the phenomenon of the self-serving bias, but they now generally agree that it is both genuine and potent. Six streams of data merge to form a powerful river of evidence.

Stream 1: Accepting more responsibility for success than failure, for good deeds than bad. Time and again experimenters have found that people readily accept credit when told they have succeeded (attributing the success to their ability and effort), yet attribute failure to such external factors as bad luck or the situation's inherent "impossibility." Similarly, in explaining their victories athletes have been observed to credit themselves, but they are more likely to attribute losses to something else: bad breaks, bad officiating, the other team's super effort. Situations that combine skill and chance (games, exams, job applications) are especially prone to the phenomenon. Winners easily attribute their success to their skill, while losers attribute their losses to chance. When I win at Scrabble it's because of my verbal dexterity; when I lose it's because "who could get anywhere with a Q but no U?"

Michael Ross and Fiore Sicoly at the University of Waterloo observed a marital version of self-serving bias.[2] They found that married people usually gave themselves more credit for such activities as cleaning the house and caring for the children than their spouses were willing to credit them for. Every night, my wife and I pitch our laundry at the bedroom clothes hamper. In the morning, one of us puts them in. Recently she suggested that I take more responsibility for this. Thinking that I already did so 75 per cent of the time, I asked her how often she thought she picked up the clothes. "Oh," she replied, "about 75 per cent of the time."

Stream 2: Favorably biased self-ratings: Can we all be better than average? On nearly any dimension that is both subjective and socially desirable, most people see themselves as better than average.[3] Most American business people, for example, see themselves as more ethical than the average American business person. Most community residents see themselves as less prejudiced than others in their communities. Most French people perceive themselves as superior to their peers in a variety of socially desirable ways. Most drivers, even among those who have been hospitalized for accidents, believe themselves to be more skillful than the average driver.

The College Board recently invited the million high-school seniors taking its aptitude test to indicate "how you feel you compare with other people your own age in certain areas of ability." Judging from the students' responses America's high-school seniors are not plagued with inferiority feelings. Sixty per cent reported themselves as better than average in "athletic ability," only 6 per cent as below average. In "leadership ability" 70 per cent rated themselves as above average, 2 per cent as below average. In "ability to get along with others," less than 1 per cent of the 829,000 students who responded rated themselves below average, 60 per cent rated themselves in the top 10 per cent, and 25 per cent saw themselves among the top 1 per cent. To paraphrase Elizabeth Barrett Browning, the question seems to be "How do I love me? Let me count the ways."

Stream 3: Self-justification: If I did it, it must be good. If we have done something undesirable that cannot be forgotten, misremembered or undone, then often we justify it. In chapter two we noted how social psychological research has established that past actions influence our current attitudes. Every time we act, we amplify the idea lying behind what we have done, especially if we feel some responsibility for having committed the act. In experiments, people who oppress someone—by delivering electric shocks, for example —tend later to disparage their victim. Such self-justification is all the more dangerous when manifest in group settings: Iran justified its taking of hostages as a just response to morally reprehensible American policies in Iran; the United States saw the moral lunacy on the other side. So everyone felt righteous, and a stand-off resulted.

Stream 4: Cognitive conceit: Belief in our personal infallibility. Researchers who study human thinking have often observed that people overestimate the accuracy of their beliefs and judgments. So consistently does this happen that one prominent researcher has referred to this human tendency as "cognitive conceit."

The I-knew-it-all-along attitude demonstrates this phenomenon. Often we do not expect something to happen until it does, at which point we overestimate our likelihood to have predicted it. Researchers have found that people who are told the outcome of an experimental or historical situation are less surprised at the outcome than people told only about the situation and its possible outcomes.[4] Indeed, almost any result of a psychological experiment can seem like common sense—after you know the result. The phenomenon can be demonstrated by giving half a group some purported psychological finding and the other half the opposite result. For example:

Social psychologists have found that, whether choosing friends or falling in love, we are most attracted to people whose traits are different from our own. There seems to be wisdom in the old saying that "opposites attract."

Social psychologists have found that, whether choosing friends or falling in love, we are most attracted to people whose traits are similar to our own. There seems to be wisdom in the old saying that "birds of a feather flock together."

Have people (1) write an explanation for whichever finding they were given, and (2) judge whether their finding is "surprising" or "not surprising." In hindsight, either result can seem obvious so that virtually all will say "not surprising." "Anyone could have told you that."

Many of the conclusions presented in this book may have already occurred to you. In retrospect, doesn't the action-attitude principle discussed in chapter two seem quite obvious? Likewise, do we really need research psychologists to rediscover the pervasiveness of pride? And let's look ahead to some of the equally obvious ideas to be examined in future chapters:

1. Human reason is sound; hence, given a reasonable exposition of Christianity, people can be held responsible for making a rational decision to choose faith (chapters four and six).

2. Paranormal happenings, documented by science, testify to realities beyond nature and even point to demonic supernatural powers (chapter five).

3. People will become most committed to those beliefs and actions they perceive to be personally rewarding (chapter seven).

4. Teaching our children to be more independent is the best way to deal with the problem of "conformity to this world" (chapter eight).

5. The greater the cohesiveness among members of a local church, the more likely they will grow in faith and practice (chapter nine).

6. The combined effects of two decades of inflation and recession have created an economic mess that has eroded our buying power (chapter ten).

7. Although we certainly note and admire physical beauty, appearance is not a major factor in our evaluations of others. Beauty is, after all, only skin deep (chapter eleven).

8. Selfishness is the overriding reason people fail to help those in distress (chapter twelve).

9. Victims of injustice typically elicit our sympathy. As Ralph Waldo Emerson once observed, "The martyr cannot be dishonored" (chapters thirteen and fourteen).

If all of these ideas seem as obvious as those presented thus far, be forewarned! The chapters that follow will challenge these myths, just as we have already sought to refute the myths that the heart must change before behavior does and that most people suffer from self-deprecation.

By the time we finish, however, their opposites may also

seem commonsensical. They are readily supported by a stockpile of ancient proverbs. Since nearly every possible outcome is conceivable, wise sayings await every occasion. Are "two heads better than one?" Or do "too many cooks spoil the broth"? Is "a penny saved a penny earned," or is it "pennywise, pound foolish"? If a social psychologist reports that separation intensifies romantic attraction, someone is sure to reply, "Of course: 'Absence makes the heart grow fonder.' " Should it turn out the reverse, the same person may remind us, "Out of sight, out of mind." No matter what happens, someone would have known it all along.

Stream 5: Unrealistic optimism: The Pollyanna syndrome. Margaret Matlin and David Stang have amassed evidence pointing to a powerful Pollyanna principle—that people more readily perceive, remember and communicate pleasant than unpleasant information.[5] Positive thinking predominates over negative thinking.

In recent research with Rutgers University students, Neil Weinstein has further discerned a tendency toward "unrealistic optimism about future life events."[6] Most students perceived themselves as far more likely than their classmates to experience positive events such as getting a good job, drawing a good salary and owning a home, and as far less likely to experience negative events such as getting divorced, having cancer and being fired. Likewise, most college students believe they will easily outlive their actuarially predicted age of death (which calls to mind Freud's joke about the man who told his wife, "If one of us should die, I think I would go live in Paris").

Stream 6: Overestimating how desirably we would act. Researchers have found that under certain conditions most people will act in rather inconsiderate, compliant or even cruel ways. When similar people are told in detail about these conditions and asked to predict how *they* would act, however, nearly all insist that their own behavior would be far more virtuous. When researcher Steven Sherman called

Bloomington, Indiana, residents and asked them to volunteer three hours to an American Cancer Society drive, only
4 per cent agreed to do so. But when a comparable group
of other residents were called and asked to predict how they
would react were they to receive such a request, almost half
predicted they would help.[7]

Other streams of evidence could be added: We more
readily believe flattering than self-deflating descriptions of
ourselves. We misremember our own past in self-enhancing
ways. We guess that physically attractive people have personalities more like our own than do unattractive people.
To summarize the argument: It's true that high self-esteem
and positive thinking are adaptive and desirable. But unless
we close our eyes to a whole river of evidence, it also seems
true that the most common error in people's self-images is
not an unrealistically low self-esteem, but rather a self-
serving bias; not an inferiority complex, but a superiority
complex. In any satisfactory theory or theology of self-
esteem, these two truths must somehow coexist.

Objections to the Self-serving Bias
Many will no doubt find this portrayal of the pervasiveness
of pride either depressing or somehow contrary to what they
have experienced and observed. Let me anticipate some of
the objections.

*I hear lots of people putting themselves down, and I'm
sometimes hampered by inferiority feelings myself.*

Let's see why this might be. First, not everyone has a self-
serving bias. Some people (women more often than men) do
suffer from unreasonably low self-esteem. For example,
several recent studies have found that while most people
shuck responsibility for their failures on a laboratory task or
perceive themselves as having been more in control than
they were, depressed people are more accurate in their self-
appraisal.[8] Sadder but wiser, they seem to be. There is also
evidence that while most people see themselves more favor-

ably than other people see them (thus providing yet another demonstration of the "normal" self-serving bias), depressed people see themselves *as* other people see them.[9] This prompts the unsettling thought that Pascal may have been right: "I lay it down as a fact that, if all men knew what others say of them, there would not be four friends in the world." Now that truly is a depressing thought.

Second, those of us who exhibit the self-serving bias (and that's most of us) may nevertheless feel inferior to certain specific individuals, especially when we compare ourselves to someone who is a step or two higher on the ladder of success, attractiveness or whatever. Thus we may *believe* ourselves to be relatively superior yet *feel* discouraged—because we fall short of certain others, or fail to fully reach our own goals.

Third, self-disparagement can be a self-serving tactic. As the French sage La Rouchefoucauld detected, "Humility is often a . . . trick whereby pride abases itself only to exalt itself later." For example, most of us have learned that putting ourselves down is a useful technique for eliciting strokes from others. We know that a remark such as "I wish I weren't so ugly" will elicit at least a "Come now. I know people who are uglier than you." Researchers have also observed that people will aggrandize their opponents and disparage or even handicap themselves as a self-protective tactic. The coach who publicly extols the upcoming opponent's awesome strength renders a loss understandable, while a win becomes a praiseworthy achievement. Thus self-disparagement can be subtly self-serving.

Perhaps all this "pride" is just an upbeat public display; underneath it people may be suffering with miserable self-images.

Actually, when people must declare their feelings publicly, they present a *more modest* self-portrayal than when allowed to respond anonymously. Other evidence also points to the conclusion that most people really do see themselves favorably and not just describe themselves that way to researchers. Self-serving bias is exhibited by children before they learn to inhibit their real feelings. And if, as many researchers believe, the self-serving bias is rooted partly in how our minds process information—I more easily recall the times I've bent over and picked up the laundry than the times I've overlooked it—then it will be an actual self-perception, more a self-deception than a lie. Consider finally the diversity of evidence that converges on the self-serving bias. If it were merely a favorability bias in questionnaire ratings, we could more readily explain the phenomenon away.

Is not the self-serving bias beneficial?

It likely is, for the same reasons that high self-esteem and positive thinking are beneficial. Some have argued that the bias has survival value—that cheaters, for example, will give a more convincing display of honesty if they believe in their honesty. Belief in our superiority can also motivate us to achieve and can sustain our sense of hope in difficult times.

However, the self-serving bias is not always beneficial. For example, in one series of experiments by Barry Schlenker at the University of Florida, people who worked with other people on various tasks claimed greater-than-average credit when their group did well and less-than-average blame when it did not.[10] If most individuals in a group believe they are underpaid and underappreciated, relative to their better-than-average contributions, disharmony and envy will likely rear their ugly heads. College presidents will readily recognize the phenomenon. If, as one survey revealed, 94 per cent of college faculty think themselves better than their average colleague, then when merit salary raises are announced and half receive an average raise or less, many will feel an injustice has been done them.

Does not the Bible portray us more positively, as reflecting God's image?

The Bible offers a balanced picture of human nature. We

are the epitome of God's creation, made in his own image, and yet we are sinful too. Two complementary truths. This chapter is affirming the sometimes understated second truth.

The experimental evidence that human reason is adaptable to self-interest strikingly parallels the Christian contention that becoming aware of our sin is like trying to see our own eyeballs. Self-serving, self-justifying biases influence the way we perceive our actions, observes the social psychologist. "No one can see his own errors," notes the psalmist (Ps 19:12 TEV). Thus the Pharisee could thank God "that I am not like other men" (Lk 18:11 RSV).

The apostle Paul must have had such self-righteousness in mind when he admonished the Philippians to "in humility count others better than yourselves" (2:3 RSV). Paul assumed that our natural tendency is the opposite, just as he assumed self-love when arguing that husbands should love their wives as their own bodies. Jesus assumed self-love too when he commanded us to love our neighbors as we love ourselves. The Bible does not teach self-love; it takes it for granted.

In the biblical view pride alienates us from God and leads us to disdain one another. It fuels conflict among individuals and nations, each of which sees itself as more moral and deserving than others. The Nazi atrocities were rooted not in self-conscious feelings of German inferiority but in Aryan pride. The conflict between Britain and Argentina in 1982 involved a small amount of real estate (the Falkland Islands) and a large amount of national pride. If you and I pride ourselves on being in the top 20 per cent of drivers, then we will likely pass off traffic safety campaigns as pertaining to those idiotic *other* drivers.

For centuries pride has been considered the fundamental sin, the deadliest of the seven deadly sins. If I seem confident about the potency of pride, it is not because I have invented a new idea but because I am simply assembling new data to reaffirm an old, old idea.

These researchers seem like killjoys. Where is there an encouraging word?

Are not the greater killjoys those who would lead us to believe that, because we're number one, we can accomplish anything? If we believe we can do anything, it means that if we don't—if we are unhappily married, poor, unemployed or have rebellious children—we have but ourselves to blame. Shame. If only we had tried harder, been more disciplined, less stupid.

To know and accept ourselves, foibles and all, without pretensions, is not gloomy but liberating. As William James noted, "To give up one's pretensions is as blessed a relief as to get them gratified." Likewise, the biblical understanding of self-affirmation does not downplay our pride and sinfulness, as some would now have us do. Recall how Jesus' Sermon on the Mount hints at the paradoxical ways by which comfort, satisfaction, mercy, peace, happiness, and visions of God are discovered: "Happy are those who know they are spiritually poor; the Kingdom of heaven belongs to them!" (Mt 5:3 TEV).

"Christian religion," said C. S. Lewis, "is, in the long run, a thing of unspeakable comfort. But it does not begin in comfort; it begins in [dismay], and it is no use at all trying to go on to that comfort without first going through that dismay."[11] In coming to realize that self-interest and illusion taint our thoughts and actions, we take the first step toward wholeness. The new insights gained from psychological research into vanity and illusion have profoundly Christian implications, for they drive us back to the biblical view of our creatureliness and spiritual poverty, the view which in our pride we are prone to deny.

Christians furthermore believe that God's grace is the key to human liberation—liberation from the need to define our self-worth solely in terms of achievements, prestige or physical and material well-being. Thus, while I can never be worthy or wise enough, I can with Martin Luther "throw myself upon God's grace." The recognition of our pride draws us to Christ and to a positive self-esteem rooted in grace. This was St. Paul's experience: "I no longer have a righteousness of my own, the kind that is gained by obeying the Law. I now have the righteousness that is given through faith in Christ, the righteousness that comes from God, and is based on faith" (Phil 3:9 TEV). The Lord of the universe loves me, just as I am.

There is indeed tremendous relief in confessing our vanity, in being known and accepted as we are. Having confessed the worst sin—playing God—and having been forgiven, we gain release, the sense of being given what we were struggling to get: security and acceptance. The feelings we can have in this encounter with God are like those we enjoy in a relationship with someone who, even after knowing our inmost thoughts, accepts us unconditionally. This is the delicious experience we enjoy in a good marriage or an intimate friendship, where we no longer feel the need to justify and explain ourselves or to be on guard, where we are free to be spontaneous without fear of losing the other's esteem. Such was the experience of the psalmist: "Lord, I have given up my pride and turned away from my arrogance. . . . I am content and at peace" (Ps 131:1-2 TEV).

What then is true humility?

First, we must recognize that the true end of humility is not self-contempt, which leaves people still concerned with themselves. To paraphrase C. S. Lewis, humility does not consist in handsome people trying to believe they are ugly or clever people trying to believe they are fools. When Muhammad Ali announced that he was the greatest, there was a sense in which his pronouncement did not violate the spirit of humility. False modesty can actually lead to an ironic pride in one's better-than-average humility. As a pastor of one modest church remarked, "We are a humble people, and we're proud of it!" (Perhaps some readers have by now similarly congratulated themselves on being unusually free of the inflated self-perception this chapter describes.)

True humility is more like self-forgetfulness than false modesty. As my colleague Dennis Voskuil writes in his book *Mountains into Goldmines: Robert Schuller and the Gospel of Success*, the refreshing gospel promise is "not that we have been freed by Christ to love ourselves, but that we have been set free from self-obsession. Not that the cross frees us *for* the ego trip but that the cross frees us *from* the ego trip."[12] This leaves people free to esteem their special talents and, with the same honesty, to esteem their neighbor's. Both the neighbor's talents and our own are recognized as gifts and, like our height, are not fit subjects for either inordinate pride or self-deprecation.

Obviously, true humility is a state not easily attained. "There is," said C. S. Lewis, "no fault which we are more unconscious of in ourselves. . . . If anyone would like to acquire humility, I can, I think, tell him the first step. The first step is to realize that one is proud. And a biggish step, too." The way to take this first step, continued Lewis, is to glimpse the greatness of God and see oneself in light of this. "He and you are two things of such a kind that if you really get into any kind of touch with Him you will, in fact, be humble, feeling the infinite relief of having for once got rid of [the pretensions which have] made you restless and unhappy all your life."[13]

4
Reasons
for
Unreason

What a piece of work is man! how
noble in reason! how infinite in
faculty!... in apprehension how
like a god!
William Shakespeare, "Hamlet"

We are the hollow men
We are the stuffed men
Leaning together
Headpiece filled with straw.
T. S. Eliot, "The Hollow Men"

COLLEGE STUDENTS listening to a lecture are told they are about to be fooled: a performer will use clever tricks to make them believe he can read their minds. A gentleman steps to the front of the room and, true to the prediction, deftly performs his sleight of mind, startling his audience volunteers with eerie revelations about their own thoughts. When the demonstration is over, the lecture hall buzzes with the remarks of excited students who believe they have witnessed a true clairvoyant.[1]

How could they have been so gullible? They had been told outright that the man had no special powers. Why, for that matter, are paranormal phenomena so attractive to credulous minds? Today's pied pipers need only pipe and people will follow as readily as ever. Devotees of Edgar Cayce and Jeane Dixon and believers in dream telepathy, out-of-body

experiences, psychokinesis, astrology, demonology, levita-
tion, reincarnation, horoscopes and ghosts are all enthralled
by mysterious phenomena that seem to defy scientific explanation.

While skepticism about extraordinary claims will sometimes prevent one from recognizing truth, the converse is
also true. A completely open mind is vulnerable to having
garbage thrown in. New research in psychology shows how
the mind collects garbage. As chapter three hinted, a basic
fact about human nature is our capacity for illusion and self-
deception. Contrary to Hamlet's paean of praise, we are not
always "noble in reason" and certainly not "infinite in
faculty."

How do we form and sustain false beliefs about ourselves
and others? And how do these illusory thinking processes
lead people to believe in paranormal phenomena? This
chapter and the next will suggest some answers.

Illusory Thinking
*Our preconceptions control our interpretations and mem-
ories.*   Recent experiments indicate that one of the most significant facts about our minds is the extent to which our
preconceived notions bias the way we view, interpret and
remember the information that comes to us. Sometimes our
minds block from our awareness something that is there, if
only we were predisposed to perceive it. While reading these
words you have probably been unaware, until this moment,
that you are looking at your nose.

Our prejudgments can also induce us to see what we already believe. Three recent psychological experiments
demonstrate the incredible biasing power of our beliefs. One,
by Charles Lord and his Stanford University colleagues,
helps explain why pondering ambiguous evidence often
fuels rather than extinguishes the fires of debate among
people who hold strongly opposing opinions.[2] They showed
college students, half of whom favored and half of whom

opposed capital punishment, two purported new research studies. One study confirmed and the other disconfirmed the students' existing beliefs about the crime-deterring effectiveness of the death penalty. Both the proponents and opponents of capital punishment readily accepted the evidence which confirmed their belief but were sharply critical of the disconfirming evidence. Showing the two sides an identical body of mixed evidence had therefore not narrowed their disagreement but increased it. Each side had perceived the evidence as supporting its belief and now believed even more strongly. Is this what happens when liberals and conservatives scrutinize the biblical evidence regarding sensitive issues such as men's and women's roles?

Researchers Craig Anderson and Lee Ross experimented with the biasing power of beliefs by planting false beliefs in people's minds and then trying to discredit those beliefs.[3] They invited their Stanford University student subjects to consider whether people who tend to take risks make good firefighters. Each participant in the experiment considered two cases. Some were shown a risk-taker as a successful firefighter and a cautious person as an unsuccessful one; others were shown cases suggesting the opposite. After forming their theory that risk-takers make better or worse firefighters, the subjects were asked to explain how they reached their conclusions. Those who were led to believe in the superiority of risk-takers typically reasoned that a willingness to risk is conducive to bravery in saving occupants from a burning building. Those who theorized the superiority of cautious people often explained that successful firefighters are careful rather than impulsive and thus less likely to risk their own and others' lives.

Once formed, each rationale could exist independent of the initial information. Thus when the subjects were informed that the cases were merely manufactured for the experiment, their new beliefs nevertheless survived mostly intact. The students retained their explanations and therefore continued to believe that risk-prone people really do make better or worse firefighters than do cautious people.

Experiments such as this have gone on to indicate that, paradoxically, the more closely we examine our theories and understand and explain how they *might* be true, the more closed we become to any information that shows otherwise. It makes one wonder: What are the consequences of creating a scientific theory, or a religious (or antireligious) doctrine, and then explaining and defending it? Do false theories and doctrines, once defended, become difficult to refute?

We sustain erroneous beliefs, too, by our tendency to re-create memories according to our present impressions. The extent to which our current beliefs control our attempts to remember the past is evident in studies of conflicting eye-witness testimonies. University of Washington psychologists Elizabeth Loftus and John Palmer showed people a film of a traffic accident and then asked them questions about what they had seen.[4] People who were asked "How fast were the cars going when they smashed into each other?" gave higher estimates than those asked "How fast were the cars going when they hit each other?" A week later they were asked whether they recalled seeing any broken glass. Although there was no broken glass in the accident, subjects who were asked the question with "smashed" were more than twice as likely to report broken glass as those asked the question with "hit."

Our preconceptions can similarly affect how we interpret and recall information from the Bible. Our prior beliefs often influence the questions we bring to the Bible and the answers we get from it. Do we want to know the biblical view of military spending? Those on both sides find the Bible supporting their position. It seems as if people are reasoning:

Military strength is right (wrong).

The Bible teaches what is right.

Therefore the Bible advocates (does not teach) military strength.

Although the biblical interpretation is not really so arbitrary as this example might suggest, never is our thinking free from the control of our assumptions. Our basic belief system is important, for it shapes our understanding of everything else.

We overestimate the accuracy of our beliefs. The intellectual conceit evident in our judgments of past knowledge (the I-knew-it-all-along phenomenon described in chapter three) extends to estimates of our current knowledge. For example, Amos Tversky at Stanford University and Daniel Kahneman at the University of British Columbia asked their subjects to estimate how many foreign cars were imported into the United States in 1968.[5] The subjects were instructed to respond with a range of figures broad enough to make it 98 per cent certain that the true figure would be included. But nearly half the time the true answer was outside the range in which they were 98 per cent confident.

This overconfidence phenomenon has become an accepted fact among researchers. If people's answers to a question are only 60 per cent correct, they will typically *feel* 75 per cent sure. Even if people feel 100 per cent sure, they still err about 15 per cent of the time. What produces this overconfidence?

Experiments such as one conducted by P. C. Wason indicate that one reason we're so sure is our reluctance to seek information that might disconfirm what we believe.[6] Wason gave British university students a three-number sequence, such as 2-4-6, and asked them to guess the rule he had used to devise the series. (The rule was simple: any three ascending numbers.) Before they submitted their answers, the subjects were allowed to generate their own sets of three numbers, and each time Wason would tell them whether or not their set conformed to his rule. Once they were certain they had the rule, they were to announce it.

The result? Seldom right but never in doubt! Twenty-three out of twenty-nine people convinced themselves of a wrong rule. They had formed an erroneous theory about the rule and then searched only for confirming evidence rather than attempting to disconfirm their intuitive hunches. Other experiments confirm that people eagerly try to verify their beliefs but are not inclined to seek evidence which might disprove their beliefs. Here again we tend to maintain false beliefs.

Anecdotes and testimonies are more persuasive than factual data. Many recent experiments have found that people's minds are swayed more by vivid examples than by reliable but abstract statistical information. For example, one recent University of Michigan study found that a single vivid welfare case had more impact on opinions about welfare recipients than did factual information running contrary to the particular case. When Ronald Reagan told audiences about the young man who used food stamps to buy an orange and then used the change to buy vodka, he exploited the power of a vivid and memorable anecdote.

Entrepreneurs exploit people's eagerness to infer general truth from a striking instance. For example, U.S. state lotteries (which typically return less than half of the billions they take in) exploit the impact of a few vivid winners. Since the statistical truth always stays buried in the back of people's minds, the system seduces them into perceiving a lottery ticket as having much greater earnings potential than it actually does.

We are often swayed by illusions of causation, correlation and personal control. The one foible of human thinking known by nearly every student of psychology is the nearly irresistible temptation to assume that when two events occur together, one has caused the other. For example, since there is a relationship between people's educational attainments and their earnings, between certain child-rearing styles and the personalities of children exposed to them, and between health practices and longevity, we too readily jump to the conclusions that education pays financial dividends, that specific parenting styles have observable effects and that changes in nutrition and exercise habits can extend life expectancy.

Sometimes a merely accidental association between two events can create a false belief that one is causing the other. Superstitious behaviors are often produced by the power of coincidence. If an act just happens to be performed before a rewarding event occurs, it is easy to get the idea that the act must have caused the reward. Of course, only occasionally will a reward indeed follow the behavior. But this erratic, "intermittent reinforcement," as experimental psychologists call it, is especially conducive to persistence. If a hungry pigeon is every so often given a food pellet regardless of what it is doing, the pigeon will often develop some ritualistic behavior and, even after the pellets have been discontinued, perform that act 10,000 times or more before quitting.[7]

Our correlation-causation confusion is compounded by our susceptibility to perceiving a correlation where none exists. Observing random events, people easily become convinced that significant relationships are occurring—when they expect to see significant relationships. As part of their research with the Bell Telephone Laboratories, William Ward and Herbert Jenkins showed people the results of a hypothetical fifty-day cloud-seeding experiment.[8] They told their subjects which of the fifty days the clouds had been seeded and which of the days it had rained. This information was nothing more than a random mix of results; sometimes it rained after seeding, sometimes it didn't. People nevertheless were convinced—in conformity with their intuitive supposition about the effects of cloud seeding—that they really had observed a relationship between cloud seeding and rain. This experiment and others like it indicate that we easily misperceive random data as confirming our beliefs. With incredible ease we make sense out of nonsense.

Our tendency to perceive random events as though they

were meaningfully related feeds the frequent illusion that chance events are subject to our personal control. Ellen Langer has demonstrated this with creative experiments on gambling behavior.[9] People were easily seduced into believing they could beat chance. If they chose a lottery number for themselves, they demanded four times as much money for the sale of their lottery ticket as did people whose number was assigned by the experimenter. If they played a game of chance against an awkward and nervous person, they were willing to bet significantly more than when playing against a dapper, confident opponent. In these and other ways Langer consistently observed that people act as if chance events were subject to their personal control.

A phenomenon called "regression toward the average" often helps create illusions of control. For example, students who score extremely high or low on a test are more likely, when retested, to fall back ("regress") toward the middle than to become even more extreme. When you're at the bottom the only way to go is up. Likewise, parents who are extremely high or low in intelligence or religiousness or political activism should expect most of their children to be less exceptional on that dimension (to "regress" toward normality).

Sometimes we recognize that events seldom continue at an extreme. Experience has taught us that when everything is going great, something will soon go wrong, and that when life is dealing us terrible blows we can usually look forward to things getting better. Often, though, we fail to recognize this regression effect. When things are exceptionally bad, whatever we try—going to a psychotherapist, starting a new diet-exercise plan, reading a self-help book—is more likely to be followed by improvement than by worsening. Thus it seems effective—even if it had no effect.

Consulting psychologists are often called when employee morale is in the pits or the sales curve is at its lowest ebb. After the consultant's suggestions are implemented, morale and sales improve, and everyone celebrates the consultant's keen insights. Similarly, a football coach who rewards his team with lavish praise and a light practice after their best game of the season and harasses them after an exceptionally bad game, may soon conclude that rewards produce poorer performance in the next game while punishments improve performance. Parents and teachers may reach the same conclusion after reacting to extremely good or bad behaviors. It seems, suggest Tversky and Kahneman, that nature operates in such a way that we often feel punished for rewarding others and rewarded for punishing them.[10]

Our erroneous beliefs may generate their own reality. There is yet another reason why false beliefs, once formed, are so resistant to correction. People's beliefs may lead them to act in ways that elicit an apparent confirmation of those beliefs.

At the University of Minnesota, Mark Snyder has conducted several experiments that demonstrate this self-fulfilling phenomenon. In one of these studies, conducted with Elizabeth Tanke and Ellen Berscheid, men students had a phone conversation with women they mistakenly thought (from having been shown a picture) were either exceptionally attractive or unattractive.[11] The women were unaware of the experiment. Analysis of just the women's comments during the conversations showed that those women who were presumed to be attractive were in fact more warm and likable on the telephone than the women who were presumed unattractive. The men's erroneous beliefs had led the women to act in ways that made the stereotypical belief—that beautiful people are desirable people —a reality.

We are misled by a number of other foibles of human thinking. Many other research findings testify to the magnitude of human folly. We often do not know why we act a certain way. We make false assertions about what we have done, why we did it and what we will do in the future. We underestimate the impact of social situations on others' behavior. We are too quick to assume that people's actions mirror their inner dispositions and attitudes. We are convinced by repeated assertions, even if we know them to be of dubious credibility. We overestimate the brilliance and competence of people who by happenstance are in positions of social power, even if we know they were assigned to that position arbitrarily.

Since we know that these errors creep into even sophisticated scientific thinking, it seems safe to conclude that none of us is exempt from them. Human nature has apparently not changed since the psalmist observed three thousand years ago that "no one can see his own errors."

Let me hasten to balance the picture lest you succumb to the cynical conclusion that all beliefs are absurd. Disciplined training of the mind—the chief aim of education—can help restrain our unbridled imagination. Indeed, it is a tribute to human wisdom that we can so elegantly analyze the imperfections of human wisdom. Were I to argue that *all* human thought is illusory, my assertion would be self-refuting, for it too would be but an illusion. It would be logically equivalent to contending that all generalizations are false, including this one. Besides, many of these errors in human intuition spring from thinking mechanisms that are generally useful. If, for example, things are sometimes subject to our control and sometimes not, we will maximize our actual control by assuming that we are in control, even if this assumption sometimes creates a superstitious illusion of control.

A Call to Humility

The seductive power of illusory thinking is enormous. It penetrates all realms of human thought, warping our perceptions of reality and prejudicing our judgments of people.

The implications of this are enormous. For theologians, it questions the assumption of human rationality that undergirds the "I choose God" theology of modern fundamental-ism—the assumption that, since our reasoning is sound, we are capable of making a rational decision for Christ. By contrast, the Reformed theology of Martin Luther and John Calvin assumes that human reason is fallen and incapable of dispassionately weighing the evidence and deciding for Christ. Thus "God chooses me" and, through the Spirit, enables my response.

For psychologists, research on illusory thinking suggests a new humility regarding the truth of our unchecked specu-lation. Since we can conceive and defend almost any theory, we must check our theories against the data of God's crea-tion. To appreciate the unreliability of armchair speculation is to admit that we need careful, scientific study of human thought and behavior.

For each of us, personally, research on human error helps us understand Jesus' admonition to "judge not." We can easily wrong people by our overconfident conclusions—say, that Billy's school problems stem from his permissive par-ents or that the quiet woman in the room next door is hostile. Nor do we need to feel intimidated by other people's cer-tainty. The belief we can hold with greatest certainty is the humbling conviction that some of our beliefs contain error. We are, after all, not gods but finite men and women. Each of us peers at reality through a glass, darkly.

If all this research reinforces Paul's declaration that hu-man wisdom is not nearly so wise as God's foolishness, well, that's OK. Faith and trust require humility. Not only is it all right to have doubts, but it is intellectual pride, even self-deification, not to grant the likelihood of error within our beliefs. Indeed, faith runs deeper than belief. Belief is founded on reason; faith is a gift of God. Even in times of deepest doubt, faith compels hope and gives the courage to risk. As P. J. Bailey wrote in "A Country Town,"
Who never doubted never half believed;
Where doubt, there truth is,—'tis her shadow.

5
Should We Believe in the Paranormal?

FOR MILLIONS OF AMERICANS, the evidence for extrasensory perception (ESP) is compelling: Jeane Dixon's gift of prophecy enabled her to foresee President Kennedy's assassination. Police psychics Dorothy Allison and Peter Hurkos solve cases that dumbfound detectives. Ordinary people have spontaneous dreams of dreaded events—only to discover that their dreams are reality. In widely publicized laboratory experiments, parapsychologists (psychologists who study "paranormal" happenings) have been astonished at gifted psychics who against all odds can discern the contents of sealed envelopes, influence the roll of a die or draw a picture of what someone else is viewing at an unknown remote location.

Why then are research psychologists overwhelmingly skeptical of all such claims? Is it simple closed-mindedness, bred by a mechanistic world view that has no room for super-natural mysteries? And how should Christians view such claims? Should we welcome them as evidence for the super-natural? Fear them as evidence of the demonic? What impli-cations do such claims have for our understanding of our-selves and others?

When confronted with extraordinary claims, we are vul-nerable to two errors. We may be either too open or too closed to the evidence. Being totally skeptical may sometimes lead us to reject the truth. The disciple Thomas found belief in Jesus' resurrection impossible until "I see in his hands the print of the nails, . . . and place my hand in his side" (Jn 20:25 RSV). During the eighteenth century scientists scoffed at the notion that meteorites had extraterrestrial origins. And twen-ty years ago how many of us would have believed claims for cosmic black holes and mysterious subatomic particles?

On the other hand, as we saw in chapter four, naiveté can make us gullible to all sorts of falsehoods. In times past people were convinced that bloodletting was therapeutic, that their personality could be predicted from the bumps on their head, and that fairies really existed. Obviously there must be reasonable efforts to validate paranormal claims. An open but critical stance is best for sifting truth from fantasy.

The Paranormal: Grounds for Skepticism

Being skeptical of paranormal events does not necessarily mean doubting the existence of a supernatural world. *Para-normal* means that which is outside the range of ordinary experience and is not scientifically explainable. *Super-natural* refers to that which is outside the physical world. The supernatural might, therefore, break into the natural world in paranormal ways. (It might also break through in normal ways.) But paranormal events as a group do not necessarily tell us anything about the supernatural world—including whether or not it exists. How should Christians, then, view the paranormal?

We can no more disprove the possibility of paranormal phenomena than we can disprove the existence of Santa Claus. But what if we could discover no reliable evidence for Santa Claus, and what if there were good reasons for thinking his existence unlikely? Would we not, pending new and convincing evidence, withhold belief? In the case of ESP (extrasensory perception), the most respectable of the paranormal claims, there are at least a half-dozen grounds for withholding belief.

1. *Parapsychology's defenders and critics agree: There has never been a reproducible psychic experiment, nor any individual who can consistently exhibit psychic ability.* British psychologist C. E. M. Hansel typifies the skepticism of most research psychologists: "After a hundred years of research, not a single individual has been found who can demonstrate ESP to the satisfaction of independent investigators."[1] Even John Beloff, past president of the Parapsychological Association, seems to agree. "No experiment showing the clear existence of the paranormal has been consistently repeated by other investigators in other laboratories."[2]

At the 1981 American Psychological Association convention one symposium examined the case for and another the case against ESP. Ironically, nearly the same words were spoken at each. Parapsychologists said that what their field needs to give it credibility is one reproducible phenomenon and a theory to explain it. The critics agreed. Parapsychology is the only discipline that (1) lacks a phenomenon and (2) lacks a theory that would lead us to expect any such phenomenon. Moreover, the critics stand ready, as they have for years, to confirm the abilities of any true psychic or to reproduce one bias-free ESP phenomenon. But parapsychologists have not been interested in sending their ESP all-star team to a psychic showdown. Sensitive psychics cannot perform under such pressure, they say; ESP is too elusive, too easily disrupted by the presence of skeptics.

2. *Spontaneous psychic experiences also fail to pass scrutiny.* Perhaps ESP is indeed not the sort of phenomenon that one repeats on demand in an experiment. Maybe it's more like the eruption of Mount St. Helens—a real and observable phenomenon, but one that occurs unbidden. If so, would-be psychics could go to the Las Vegas and Atlantic City craps tables, which skim off but 1.4 per cent of the money bet. Their motive could be charitable—say, to divert money from the gambling industry into the hands of hungry people. And they don't have to bet on demand. They could just stand there and wait for spontaneous premonitions to erupt. A psychic need only beat chance by 3 per cent to clear the same profit as the house usually does. But the casinos continue to operate, showing, as always, the expected return.

Or consider the predictions of would-be seers. Not only did Jeane Dixon never predict anything so precise as "John Kennedy will be elected and then assassinated," but she changed her mind before his election, saying that Richard Nixon would be elected in 1960. More recently she predicted that Pope Paul would enjoy a year of good health (he died), that the Panama Canal treaties would be defeated in Congress (they were approved), that Marie Osmond would not marry (two months later she did), and that Ted Kennedy would be elected President in 1980 (he wasn't). No celebrated psychic has been shown to have a better-than-guessing batting average. Yet the money continues to roll in from those who love to believe.

Do the spontaneous premonitions of ordinary people fare better? How about our dreams? Do they foretell the future, or do they only seem to because we are more likely to remember or reconstruct dreams that seem to come true? A half century ago, when the Lindbergh baby was kidnaped and murdered but before the body was discovered, two Harvard psychologists invited the public to send in their dream reports concerning the whereabouts of the child.[3] Of the 1,300 dream reports received, all spontaneously experienced by people who felt they might have significance, how many accurately perceived the child as dead? Five per cent.

3. *Among professional psychics is a long history of fraud.* For years, stage performers of ESP have been convincing audiences of their wondrous powers. The most notorious of these have been debunked, often by magicians who do not take kindly to those who exploit their magical art and distort people's understanding of reality. Magician James Randi, for example, has duplicated the feats of stage psychics and offered $10,000 to anyone who can demonstrate psychic powers before a group of informed experts like himself.

Is there in all the world anyone who can read others' minds, move remote objects or perform any of the feats described at the beginning of this chapter? Randi's offer has been well publicized for nearly twenty years. On occasion he has even surrendered his cashier's check to an impartial jury which had to judge whether the psychic feat was actually performed as claimed under the agreed-upon conditions. As of this writing, fifty-seven have submitted to a test. All have failed.

Honest parapsychology researchers have at times been deceived by subjects, such as spoon-bender Uri Geller, who were later discovered to be using trickery. To demonstrate the vulnerability of scientists untrained in magic, two teenage magicians in 1979 approached Washington University's newly funded parapsychology laboratory. Over the next three years the two defied the laws of nature by projecting mental images onto film, effortlessly bending keys and spoons, causing clocks to slide across a table, affecting objects in sealed jars and performing other such marvelous feats. Although the researcher who directs the laboratory had been cautioned against trickery and reminded of the need to have magicians present, he ignored the warnings and proclaimed that "these two kids are the most reliable of the people that we've studied."[4] Having demonstrated the need for tighter safeguards in parapsychological research, the two in 1983 appeared at a news conference to reveal their psychic sham. Their many psychic feats had been nothing more than magic stunts.

4. *The fact that most people believe in ESP, and even believe that they have personally experienced it, is now understandable.* Some people wonder: If ESP does not exist, then why in one recent national poll did 64 per cent of college graduates say they believe in it? And why, in another national survey, did 58 per cent of Americans claim to have "personally experienced" ESP?

In chapter four we described the explosion in our knowledge of how people form false beliefs. We noted the evidence that people's minds are as much swayed by vivid anecdotes as by dry facts. This vulnerability to the dramatic helps explain why even forewarned college students may misinterpret a magician's tricks as genuine ESP.[5]

Moreover, people fail to recognize chance events for what they are. Ordinary events seem extraordinary. Given the billions of events occurring in the world each day, some incredible coincidences are bound to happen. Here is my favorite: The King James Bible was completed when William Shakespeare was forty-six years old. In Psalm 46, the forty-sixth word is "shake," and the forty-sixth word from the end (ignoring Selah, a symbol) is "spear." (Perhaps it is even more incredible that someone discovered this!) When "police psychics" fire hundreds of predictions, their verbal shotguns are bound to score a few "amazing" (coincidental) hits, which the media are only too happy to report. However, the unglamorous fact is that researchers have found that police psychics do no better than could you or I, given the same information about a case. After the Atlanta police department had scrutinized the psychic visions of Dorothy Allison and more than five hundred others in their search for the child killer, it remained for dogged police work to solve the case.

Other times, what seems like ESP is neither that nor a sheer coincidence. Driving down the highway a husband remarks to his wife, "I wonder what ever happened to Steve Thompson?" Astonished, his wife replies, "I was just about to say the same thing!" Both are unaware of what stimulated their common memory of Steve, perhaps a voice like his on the radio moments before or an image from a passing billboard. Given how difficult it is for people to assess the mysterious workings of their minds, they naturally attribute such shared thoughts to mental telepathy.

As we saw in chapter four, one of the most startling facts about the human mind is the extent to which preconceived notions bias the way information is interpreted and remembered. Our prejudgments can, for example, induce us to see and recall what we already believe. Many psychic predictions are vague enough to allow a variety of later interpretations. Most people will later, once they know the facts, tend to recall and interpret the prediction as fulfilled, matching the precise occurrence with the one way the general prediction could fit. Even when shown purely random events, people in experiments easily become convinced that significant relationships are occurring—if they expect to see them. Conversely, premonitions that clearly fail are usually forgotten. The 95 per cent whose dreams incorrectly anticipated the fate of the kidnaped Lindbergh baby surely forgot their dreams sooner than did the 5 per cent whose premonitions were accurate.

Researchers have used these deficiencies in human intuition to manufacture false beliefs in ESP. Fred Ayeroff and Robert Abelson asked 100 Yale students to try to transmit mentally one of five possible symbols to another student, who would guess what was being transmitted.[6] When the students were further drawn into the drama of experiment by choosing their own symbols and being given a warm-up period, more than 50 per cent of the time they felt confident that they were experiencing ESP. But their actual ESP success rate was just about what chance would give: 20 per cent.

These mental processes are some of the ingredients in human nature's recipe for convincing us of phenomena that may not exist. Indeed, these illusory thinking tendencies are so powerful that whether psychic powers exist or not, it seems almost inevitable that humanity would convince itself of them.

5. *The accumulating evidence that the mind is dependent on the brain works against the presumption that mind can function (or travel) separate from brain.* Some Christian writers have touted ESP as proof of a nonmaterial essence in human nature, but books and articles along this line often show an unawareness of both the scientific status of ESP and of the emerging biblical and scientific consensus that human nature is a bonded mind-body unity. Investigations of the correspondence between our brain states and our emotions, thoughts and actions indicate that the mind is linked to the body as closely as is a telephone message to the electrical events in the phone line. This modern view parallels the ancient wholistic view of the Hebrew people, expressed in the radical Christian hope of a resurrected mind-body unit. In both views, the idea that human minds could travel and communicate independent of human bodies has become as questionable as the idea that telephone messages could travel independent of the phone equipment.

6. *The Bible counsels us to be skeptical of those who claim godlike abilities.* We humans have always had a hard time accepting our finiteness. In the creation story, humanity's fall occurred when man and woman denied their human limitations. Today occultists and other believers in ESP are again proclaiming the human potential to mimic God: to be omniscient—reading others' minds and knowing the future; to be omnipresent—traveling out of body and viewing events in remote locations; to be omnipotent—moving or even destroying objects with the mind's hidden powers. Science, in questioning such self-deifying claims, sides with biblical faith, which proclaims that our hope lies not in ourselves,

our mental powers or the immortality of our disembodied minds, but in a Being who created and accepts our limits and who promises to resurrect us. Not surprisingly, surveys reveal that people who have given up believing in such a Being are more likely to find paranormal claims credible. As George Tyrell declared, "If [people's] craving for the mysterious, the wonderful, the supernatural, be not fed on true religion it will feed itself on the garbage of any superstition that is offered to it." When people no longer wrestle with the real mysteries of religious faith, they become susceptible to the unsubstantiated mysteries of pseudoscience.

For all these reasons, *open skepticism* seems the informed response to the modern avalanche of psychic claims. Most scientists and magicians keep themselves open to belief should any demonstrable phenomenon be discovered. Christians, too, must keep their eyes and ears open to the full potential of God's creation. Are proponents of ESP equally willing to say what would cause them to question their belief? What would it take? How many failed attempts to demonstrate a reproducible psychic phenomenon? How many years of casinos getting their expected returns? How many psychic hoaxes? How many failures to pass Randi's $10,000 challenge? How much evidence concerning the dependence of mind on brain? How much biblical revelation about our human limits?

The Supernatural: Can a Skeptic Believe?

I have often been asked, How can you question these paranormal claims and then turn right around and believe other equally paranormal (beyond-the-normal, unexplainable) claims? After all, aren't the existence of God, the resurrection of Jesus, and life after death also paranormal claims? Consider three replies.

First, the question is no different from asking, How can one disbelieve in Santa Claus, yet believe in Jesus? All of us believe some things while disbelieving others. Belief in some claims that are not scientifically confirmed does not require believing all unproven claims. Faith in Christ is not blind credulity.[7]

Second, not all truth is scientific. The beauty of a Mozart piano concerto or the love of a father for his son are not easily measured by the tools of science. Nonetheless, they are real. History, philosophy and theology are disciplines which also offer insight into truth. Yet they are not scientific. If evidence from such sources can be amassed to substantiate certain untestable religious claims, doubting the claims may be the more difficult position to defend.

Third, a clear difference lies between the easily testable claims of ESP and the not-scientifically-testable claims that God exists. Take, for example, those who claim to see colored auras surrounding people's bodies. Magician Randi proposes a simple test of this claim. His typical conversation with such psychics goes something like this:

Randi: Do you see an aura around my head?

Psychic: Sure!

Randi: Can you still see the aura if I put this magazine in front of my face?

Psychic: Of course.

Randi: Then if I were to step behind a wall barely taller than I am, you could determine my location from the aura visible above my head, right?

Randi reports that no aura-seer has yet agreed to take this simple test. Just because most Christian beliefs are not similarly refutable does not prove that they are true. It simply means that they are a different type of claim. It is true, however, that (1) they have not been refuted, (2) they are essentially congenial with what we know from extrabiblical sources about human nature, and (3) they are defensibly worthy of our commitment.

Fourth, the Bible warns us against being misled by self-professed psychics. The Mosaic law was definite: "Don't let your people practice divination or look for omens or use spells or charms, and don't let them consult the spirits of the dead" (Deut 18:10-11 TEV). In Isaiah the Lord scoffs at the Babylonians' pagan beliefs: "Keep all your magic spells and charms. . . . You are powerless in spite of the advice you get. Let your astrologers come forward and save you. . . . They will be like bits of straw" (Is 47:12-14 TEV).

True, the Bible does offer its own paranormal claims— Joseph's predictive dreams, Elisha's dividing the Jordan River with his cloak, Jesus' miracles. But the action is attributed to divine power, not human skill or even human manipulation of divine power. The will and the act are God's. As for biblical prophecy, much of it was less a prediction of the future than an inspired understanding of where the present course was leading. A modern Amos might not name the date of the world's next war, but he would discern that if the nations of the world do not turn from their wicked ways a war without winners is likely. While much Old Testament prophecy *was* clearly predictive of the future, Moses counseled a scientific attitude toward predictions: "If a prophet speaks in the name of the LORD and what he says does not come true, then it is not the LORD's message" (Deut 18:22 TEV).

This is the same spirit that Carl Sagan echoes today: "Skeptical scrutiny is the means, in both science and religion, by which deep insights can be winnowed from deep nonsense." Skepticism protects us from those who would exploit us. Jim Jones seduced people into his cult partly by using psychic fakery to convince them of his extraordinary gifts.[8] Pseudoscience and the occult always threaten genuine science and religion by distracting people from pursuing truth and godly living.

Skepticism can be carried to an extreme or degenerate into a cold, closed-minded cynicism. Henrik Ibsen's play *The Wild Duck* portrays the potentially harmful effects of destroying people's comforting illusions without replacing them with something better. But skepticism can also be a healthy part of the search for truth. Those who would "worship God with their minds" search for truth, believing that it is better to hope for things genuine than things unreal, better to base our lives on the rock of reality than the sands of illusion. Proper skepticism acknowledges mystery. Clearing the decks of pseudomysteries can free us to ponder the genuine mysteries of faith and life.

Christians should welcome all evidence for the existence of a supernatural world. Unfortunately fakes and well-intentioned but mistaken people have sometimes smeared all who believe in the supernatural. The attempts at proof (including those of many Christians) have often been either uninformed or tended to aggrandize the performer rather than bring us into the presence of the Holy One. Such people tend to believe that we can force the hand of psychic forces or divine power by rituals, powers of concentration or prayers prayed in utter belief (that is, human effort to have faith). But a Christian view is that God's power is for him alone to control. We cannot manipulate him. It is our role to seek to live obediently in his will.

On this much the believers and skeptics of the paranormal agree: at issue is not just whether ESP exists but our whole understanding of human nature. It is the basic question raised in this part of this book: How are we to believe what we believe, especially about ourselves and others? Do we possess divine, supernatural attributes? Or are we finite creatures of the One who declares, "I am God, and there is none like me"? Judaism and Christianity have historically maintained that we do not inherently possess extraordinary supernatural powers. We are the creatures of the one great supernatural being, the Creator God who occasionally gives special gifts to individuals for the good of the body. An inflated self-image tempts us to deny our limits and see ourselves as beings who possess God's supernatural powers.

So, no, Virginia, there is no Santa Claus, and no, human

beings appear not to have divine powers. But don't worry. It's okay. We can have dignity without having deity. The One who is deity has redeemed us and is restoring us to creaturely dignity.

Part II
Influencing

"YOU ARE THE SALT of the earth, ... the light of the world."
"Go therefore and make disciples of all nations." "Do not
be conformed to this world." "Obey God rather than men"
(Mt 5:13-14; 28:19; Rom 12:2; Acts 5:29 RSV). To be in the
world but not of it: that is God's call. To influence the world
but not be tainted by it. Social influence—how we shape and
are shaped by our social worlds—is the focus of Part II.

Sometimes our communication has a disappointing impact. Chapter six asks, What factors make for memorable,
persuasive communication? How may those who teach,
speak or write do so with greatest influence? And what can
all of us do to get the most from what we hear and read? We
will examine principles of effective communication and
consider how they may be applied within the Christian
community.

While chapter six deals with the form of our messages, chapter seven concerns their content. To shape attitudes and behavior we frequently rely on rewards. In fact, the Christian message itself is often presented in terms of what faith will do for us. While rewards can be effective in changing behavior, they may have hidden costs. The frequent appeal to personal need and the ready use of rewards in our proclamation of the gospel may not only foster self-centered religion but in the long run undermine the message's credibility.

Chapter eight moves on to how the world can influence us. While we want to be shaped by God, others may influence our thoughts and actions more than we are willing to admit. In some cases, social pressure leads us to yield against our better judgment; with Peter we may say by our actions that we "do not know the man" (Mt 26:69-75 RSV). In other cases conformity extends beyond our actions to the core of our beliefs and values. Greater independence is not the solution to conformity. This chapter proposes a solution both biblically and sociologically sound.

Within God's community there are problems, too. In chapter nine we will see how the desire to maintain harmony can become so strong that it results in a loss of critical judgment. Fear of conflict can lead to "groupthink." When groupthink hits the church, doctrine and practice are not critically examined, and we grow neither in our understanding of God's Word nor in its application to the problems of contemporary living. Here we try to answer, What causes groupthink in the church, and how can it be cured?

6
Is Anyone
Getting
the Message?

A YOUNG COUPLE, Martha and Leon, happily file out from Sunday worship at Faith Church, congratulating the pastor for his fine message on Christian love. Later that week when her friend Sally, who was ill on Sunday, asks her about the sermon, Martha can recall little of its content. Perhaps, Sally surmises, she is just upset and distracted by how unloving Leon has been lately.

Is this typical or atypical of the impact of sermons? Those of us who teach or preach become so easily enamored by our spoken words that we are tempted to overestimate their power. Ask college students what aspect of their college experience has been most valuable, or what they remember from their freshman year, and few will recall the brilliant lectures which their faculty gave.

Would the same be true of people reflecting on their church

experience? A recent award-winning study by University of California psychologist Thomas Crawford indicates that sermons sometimes have surprisingly little impact.[1] Crawford and his associates went to the homes of people from twelve churches shortly before and after they heard sermons opposing racial bigotry and injustice. When asked during the second interview whether they had heard or read anything about racial prejudice or discrimination since the previous interview, only 10 per cent spontaneously recalled the sermon. When the remaining 90 per cent were asked directly whether their minister "talked about prejudice or discrimination in the last couple of weeks," more than 30 per cent denied hearing such a sermon. It is hardly surprising that the sermons had so little impact on racial attitudes!

When you stop to think about it, the preacher has so many hurdles to surmount, it's no wonder that preaching so often fails to affect our actions. As figure 2 indicates, the preacher must deliver a message which not only gets our attention but is understandable, persuasive, memorable and likely to compel action. Our concern here is with neither theological content nor oratorical style, but with how to create and receive a memorable, persuasive message. What factors make for effective communication? How might ministers apply these

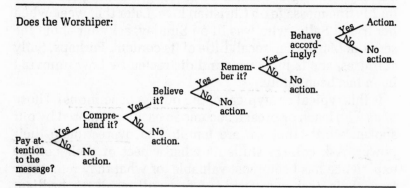

Figure 2. *Requirements for an effective sermon. Adapted from the writings of Yale University social psychologist William McGuire.*

factors in the construction of more potent messages? For that matter, how might any of us who teach, speak or write do so with greatest effect? Finally, what can we lay people do to receive maximum benefit from what we hear and read? Recent research has revealed five keys to help us answer these questions.

Five Keys

1. *Vivid, concrete examples are more potent than abstract information.* We noted in chapter four that our judgments and attitudes are often more swayed by specific illustrations than by abstract assertions of general truth. For example, research studies show that a few good testimonials usually have more impact than statistically summarized data from dozens of people. Not surprisingly, the mastectomies performed on Betty Ford and Happy Rockefeller did more to increase visits to cancer detection clinics than all the reports of the National Institute of Health. Likewise, viewing the movie *Jaws* gave many swimmers a fear of sharks which no factual data on actual shark attacks could eliminate.

Concrete examples are not only more compelling, but they are also better remembered. Joanne Martin and her colleagues at Stanford University have observed that concepts are better remembered when concrete details are included.[2] They had Coast Guard recruits read one of the following paragraphs and then write everything they could recall from it. Those who read the following abstract description of what happens when a Coast Guard regulation is broken recalled only 27 per cent of the words afterward:

If a new Seaman Apprentice breaks a Coast Guard regulation, and this frequently happens, then he usually gets caught. If he gives serious personal excuses for what he did, then the Executive Officer usually will not accept such excuses. Executive Officers usually refer the matter to mast. Usually in these cases the defendant is found guilty. If the new Seaman Apprentice is found guilty, then he will be sentenced with a variety of punishments.

Other recruits read a concrete instance of this information:
Robert Christensen, a new Seaman Apprentice, reported
for duty on the CG Cutter Seagull two days late. His excuse
for being late was that his father had become seriously ill
while he was visiting home. The Executive Officer did not
accept his excuse. He referred the matter to mast. Seaman
Apprentice Christensen was found guilty and sentenced
to one month extra duty, a $50 fine each month for two
months, and one month restriction.

Those given this anecdotal paragraph not only recalled
almost twice as many words as those given the abstract paragraph; they were about twice as likely to recall concepts such
as "found guilty."

No experienced writer will be surprised by this finding.
As William Strunk and E. B. White assert in their classic *The
Elements of Style*, "If those who have studied the art of writing are in accord on any one point, it is on this: the surest way
to arouse and hold the attention of the reader is by being specific, definite, and concrete. The greatest writers—Homer,
Dante, Shakespeare—are effective largely because they deal
in particulars."[3] Preachers and teachers should do the same,
and so should we listeners, by conjuring up our own examples when the speaker begins to get abstract.

However, a sermon is never just a string of unrelated examples; the preacher aims to communicate a basic point. We
might say that theological truth is to a good sermon what the
base of an iceberg is to its tip. Jesus' vivid parables, for example, embodied basic truths in memorable pictures. And what
pastor has not received compliments from adults for a simple
but concrete children's sermon? The children may have been
unable to grasp the analogy being drawn, but the adults un-
derstood and remembered it. This illustrates the power of
principle number one: vivid, concrete examples are more
potent than abstract information.

2. *Messages which relate to what people already know* or

have experienced are more easily remembered. Public speaking experts have long supposed this to be true. Aristotle urged speakers to adapt the message to their audiences. Experimental psychologists have confirmed the point; messages that are unrelated to people's existing ideas or experiences are difficult to comprehend and are quickly forgotten. This paragraph, from an experiment by John Bransford and Marcia Johnson, is an example of such an "unattached" message:

> The procedure is actually quite simple. First you arrange things into different groups. Of course, one pile may be sufficient depending on how much there is to do. . . . After the procedure is completed, one arranges the materials into different groups again. Then they can be put into their proper places. Eventually they will be used once more and the whole cycle will then have to be repeated. However, that is a part of life.

When Bransford and Johnson had people read this paragraph as you just did, without connecting it to anything they already knew about, little of it was remembered. When people were told that the paragraph was about sorting laundry, something familiar to them, they remembered much more of it—as you probably could now if you reread it.[4]

When a message builds on our knowledge and experience, we not only more easily understand and remember it, but we are also more likely to recall it when that knowledge or experience comes again into consciousness. In other words, a message that is hooked to some cue—something we will think about or experience again—is more likely to come to mind in the future. When the cue pops up, it may call to mind the message associated with it. For example, one preacher said that much American religion was like waiting room Muzak—bland and soothing. A year after this "Sound of Muzak" sermon was preached, we found ourselves eating dinner in a room with music softly playing in the background. Someone noticed the music—and recalled the sermon.

If preachers and teachers are to build their messages on
their people's knowledge and experience, then they must
know their people. One advantage which local pastors,
teachers and youth workers have over mass-media preachers is a more intimate knowledge of the experiences of their
people. When pastors systematically seek out their parishioners for deep conversation, they are engaging in sermon
preparation as well as pastoral ministry. When we parishioners freely talk to our pastors about our concerns, we help
them know what sermon themes will touch us as well as
what we need. This is another implication of principle number two: messages which relate to what people already know
or have experienced are most easily remembered.

3. *Spaced repetition aids memory.* As every student of
human learning knows well, we remember information
much better if it is presented to us repeatedly, especially if
the repetitions are spaced over time rather than grouped together. Experimental psychologist Lynn Hasher has found
that repeated information is also more credible.[5] When statements, such as "The largest museum in the world is the
Louvre in Paris," were repeatedly presented, people rated
them as more likely to be true than when they had been
shown infrequently. Social psychologists have uncovered a
parallel phenomenon: repeated presentation of a stimulus
—whether a human face, a Chinese character or a piece of
unfamiliar music—generally increases people's liking of it.

Speakers can capitalize on this finding that repetition,
especially spaced repetition, makes messages more memorable and appealing. When preparing a talk or sermon they
might ask themselves, What do I most want people to remember from this? They can then repeat that one key idea numer-
ous times. (We suspect that a little informal testing of parishioners' recall would reveal that few people can recall the
main points of the last three-point sermon they heard.) Given
the limitations of human memory, the advice of Henry Grady
Davis appears sound: A sermon should be "the embodiment

of one vigorous idea." Perhaps this could even be taken a step further: that idea should be embodied in the whole worship service—the Scriptures, music, prayers and closing charge to the congregation. As parishioners we should look for a unifying theme, or at least identify one idea in every service that is significant for us.

Sometimes the key idea can be captured in a single statement or pithy saying that becomes the trunk of a talk or sermon, unifying the illustrative branches which grow from it. Who can forget the refrain in Martin Luther King Jr.'s "I Have a Dream" sermon? Principle number three bears repeating: spaced repetition aids retention.

4. *Active listening aids memory and facilitates attitude change.* People remember information best when they have actively processed it, that is, when they have put it in their own words. When we read or hear something that prompts a thought of our own, we will often more readily remember our thought than the information which prompted it. University of Toronto psychologists Norman Slamecka and Peter Graf recently found that people can more easily recall information they have produced than information they have been told to memorize.[6] For example, people who were given the word *rapid* and were asked to produce a synonym beginning with the letter "f" later remembered the word *fast* better than did people asked directly to remember *fast*.

Not only do we better remember information we produce ourselves, but our attitudes are also more likely to be changed by that information. For example, social psychologists have found that passive exposure to information, through reading or listening, has less effect on people's attitudes than information they got through active participation in a group discussion. Other research confirms that when we passively learn something our attitudes toward it usually do not change much. When we are stimulated into restating information in our own terms, we are much more likely to remember it *and* to be persuaded by it.

Preachers, teachers and even parents may fail to recognize that their spoken words are more prominent to them (as active speakers) than to their passive listeners. Parents are often amazed at their children's capacity to ignore them. If, instead of constant harping, the parent gently asks the child to restate the request ("Andy, what did I ask you to do?"), the child's act of verbalizing the request will make him or her more aware of it. Mister Rogers, the television friend of pre-schoolers, applies this principle by asking a question and then saying nothing for a few moments, allowing children to answer for themselves. Preachers would be well advised to do likewise, pausing after giving an instruction or raising a thought-provoking question.

People who run an idea through their minds are also more likely to *act* on it. This is implied by research on the impact of participating in a public opinion poll, conducted by Michael Traugott and John Katosh of the University of Michigan.[7] Those who rehearse their political attitudes by participating in a pre-election survey more often act on them by voting in the election than do people not selected for the survey. For this reason, too, listeners should be provoked to repeat and restate what they hear.

As listeners we can discipline ourselves to listen actively. Taking notes on a sermon, as any serious student does in class, forces us to repeat and restate its main points. So does discussing it with someone else. William James made the point eighty years ago: "No reception without *reaction*, no impression without correlative expression—this is the great maxim which the teacher ought never to forget."[8] James anticipated principle number four: active listening aids memory and facilitates attitude change.

5. *Attitudes and beliefs are shaped by action.* If social psychological research has established anything, it is, as noted in chapter two, that our actions influence our attitudes. Every time we act, we amplify the idea lying behind what we have done, especially when we feel some responsi-

bility for having committed the act. It seems that we are as likely to believe in what we have stood up for as to stand up for what we believe. Moreover, this principle is paralleled by the biblical idea that growth in faith is a *consequence of obedient action* as well as its source.

The implication of this "attitudes follow actions" principle is clear: a message is most likely to stimulate faith if it calls forth a specific action. The effective talk or sermon will not leave people wondering what to do with it. It will suggest specific actions, or it will stimulate listeners to form their own plan of action. "How will 'Love your neighbor' affect you?" the speaker might ask. "Who are you going to phone or visit this week?"

Just Remember

These five research-based principles for constructing a memorable and persuasive message can be wedded to a variety of speaking styles and theological orientations. Just remember:

1. Vivid, concrete _examples_ are more potent than abstract information.

2. Messages which relate to what people already _know_ or have _experienced_ are most easily remembered.

3. Spaced _repetition_ aids retention.

4. Active _listening_ aids memory and facilitates attitude change.

5. Attitudes and beliefs are shaped by _action_.

And if you really want to remember these principles, look away and repeat them in your own words. Better yet, tell someone else about them or pick out one or two and think about how you might apply them to the next talk you prepare or hear.

The Word of God has power to change lives (Heb 4:12) but "how are they to hear without a preacher?" (Rom 10:14 RSV). The charge to communicate compels us to do it effectively.

7
The Cost of Rewards

MOST PEOPLE PAY TO play golf; a few play for the pay. Some grow roses for the sheer fun of it; others do so to earn a living. My kindergarten daughter can hardly wait for the weekend to end—with Monday returns the excitement of school! But my fifth- and seventh-grade sons are already counting the days until vacation. A colleague finds his daily seven-mile run exhilarating. My painful two miles keeps me in shape.

Means versus Ends: Why Do It?
People engage in the same action for different reasons. What one person finds to be an end in itself, another sees as merely a means to an end. *Intrinsically motivated* action is done for its own sake. The task is inherently interesting, challenging and enjoyable. *Extrinsically motivated* action is performed with some other goal in mind. The reward—a gold star, a

dollar bill, a promotion—is not built into the activity itself.

Educators, employers and advertisers recognize the value of intrinsic motivation. Children who find challenge and satisfaction in study not only learn more, they are fun to teach. Employees who enjoy their work not only produce a better product, they require less surveillance. And consumers who are convinced a product is the best on the market don't need rebates.

The problem is that some activities are simply not intrinsically challenging or satisfying. Yet they must be performed. Other activities may have the potential of bringing satisfaction, but people simply refuse to attempt them. In both cases, introducing a little extrinsic motivation works miracles. In fact, it is one of psychology's most firmly established principles. The promise of reward or threat of punishment is often the easiest and most effective way of influencing someone. The offer of $5 for each passing grade on a report card can produce a sudden change in a child's study habits. Placing employees on a piecework schedule of pay may dramatically increase their productivity. And our family's choice of toothpaste is readily bent by the size of the manufacturer's rebate offer. The principle works. Extrinsic rewards motivate people. We use them and respond readily to them.

The distinction between intrinsic and extrinsic motivation has been important in the psychology of religion as well. In his book *The Individual and His Religion*, Gordon Allport attempted to explain how religion functions in people's lives. He distinguished between two kinds of religious outlooks or orientations which he later labeled the extrinsic and the intrinsic.[1] For some, said Allport, religious activity is extrinsically motivated. It is a way to get such things as social status, business contacts, self-justification or security. Extrinsic people tend to make statements like "A primary reason for my interest in religion is that my church is a congenial social activity." For others, reasoned Allport, religious experience is an end in itself. They find meaning and purpose in their religious commitment, and their faith provides direction to all of life. These intrinsically motivated people are likely to say, "My religious beliefs are what really lie behind my whole approach to life."

Allport's distinction parallels what the Old Testament prophets Hosea and Amos argued centuries ago. Distinguishing between religious ceremonies and righteousness, between burnt offerings and the knowledge of God, between sacrifices and steadfast love, the prophets sharply contrasted religion as ritual with religion as loyalty. In more contemporary terms we often distinguish between "nominal" and "committed" Christians. For some, faith is superficial and isolated from most of life. For others it's the moving force. Even within the church, where you'd expect everyone to agree that religious faith is central, differences exist. For some worship and service are a burden. Others experience their responsibilities to God as more than a duty: they find joy and satisfaction in meeting them.

Rewards in the Church

Just as teachers and employers in schools and industry recognize the value of intrinsic motivation, so do most of those directing evangelism and education programs in the church. They also know how difficult it is to foster! As has happened in other settings, they resort to extrinsic motivators.

Two recent experiences remind me of how we apply the reward principle in church. Just a week ago my younger son returned from his first Sunday-school class of the season. He announced that his teacher has promised a "nice prize" to each student who maintains perfect attendance. And for the last several Thursdays we have received tracts distributed by another local church, apparently as part of their evangelism program. Each has been a variation on the theme of how those who repent will escape hell's eternal torture and will instead enjoy heaven's lavish rewards.

The use of rewards to shape behavior in the church has a long history. Benjamin Franklin reported that a Navy chaplain improved sailors' attendance at worship services by serving a round of rum after each service.[2] Having grown up near Chicago, I recall how local churches operated a mission on Skid Row. Fortunately, not rum but coffee and sandwiches were used on Friday nights to attract alcoholics. However, the down-and-outers were required first to sit through a lengthy sermon calling them to repentance.

In *The Human Reflex* Rodger Bufford reviews the variety of ways the reward principle has been used in Christian education and evangelism. The Bible Memory Association promotes memorization of Scripture verses by awarding prizes at three-week intervals for successful work. Each individual pays a small fee to participate and then memorizes a given number of Bible verses focused on a particular theme. In addition to the prizes awarded every three weeks, children who master an entire book may attend summer camp at a reduced rate. Bufford cites how one Christian family adopted a similar approach, making dessert with the evening meal contingent on the recital of Bible verses!

Social rewards are frequently used as motivators in church programs. Learners can take part in some fun activity with others if they successfully complete the Sunday-school lesson or Bible study assignment. So teachers may tell their young students, "When you have all finished in your workbooks, we will play a game." Women in one carefully structured Bible study program were told they could go to the group's monthly social only if they had completed the work for their weekly Bible study classes. The Christian Service Brigade program makes special outings contingent on successful achievement in a variety of areas, including Bible study.

Social attention and approval are powerful reinforcers for both children and adults. Charismatic leaders on the fringe of Christianity use them effectively. A potential convert attending the group's meeting for the first time finds herself the object of "love bombing." She feels warm and accepted as the leader presents the group as a closely knit family united by ties of affection and common purpose. The invitation to become part of the family proves irresistible.

Finally, perhaps most significantly, the Christian message itself has been presented only in terms of its instrumentality. Look what becoming a Christian will do for you! Ministers, teachers and missionaries are encouraged to fit their presentations to the needs of the audience. Learn where your people are at and preach accordingly! If their problem is physical illness, present a God who takes away suffering. Do they feel inferior? Preach a God who accepts them as they are. If they have recently suffered economic loss, they need a God of power and success. Just listen to the Sunday television preachers. Faith produces deliverance from every imaginable human problem.

Why Not Use Them?

The strongest argument against using rewards in the church is that it fosters self-centered religion. The worship of God and service to others recede into the background while our own needs move to the fore. The teaching of Scripture "to lose self" is muffled. The message that God as God has the right to our loyalty and that we are obligated to obey is not heard. No longer do we hear Christ say, "Any of you who does not give up everything he has cannot be my disciple" (Lk 14:33 NIV).

The objection is valid. Some within the Christian community seem strangely unaware that Christian faith is anything more than the means of satisfying their personal need. God apparently exists only to please people, not the other way around.

Others say that while true faith does involve the worship of God, rewards and appeals to personal needs can motivate first steps in that direction. People must find that God meets their needs before they are able or willing to commit their lives in obedient service to him. Jesus is first Savior, then Lord. Sunday television preachers sometimes argue, "We first grab their attention. Later we gain the commitment."

Such thinking, that extrinsic rewards enhance intrinsic motivation, used to be generally accepted in psychology. Children given quarters for completing their math assignments should eventually discover that math is indeed worth studying. Adults given electric shock for smoking should find clear lungs and a fresh, unparched mouth so delightful that they give up the habit permanently.

The Hidden Costs

Recent research reveals, however, that rewards do not always have such positive consequences. Although rewards shape behavior, they have "hidden costs."[3] Often their effects evaporate soon after they are terminated. Worse, they sometimes undermine the very intrinsic motivation they were supposed to engender.

The detrimental effect is clearly seen in the results of one study of preschool children.[4] Half the children were induced to work on a set of plastic jigsaw puzzles with the promise of an even more rewarding activity later. Others were not promised the more enjoyable activity. After playing with the puzzles for some time, all the children were allowed to engage in the more rewarding activity. Some days later the kids were turned loose on the puzzles. Those who had earlier worked on the puzzles in order to gain the more rewarding activity now played with them less. By bribing the children to play with the puzzles the experimenter had turned play into work.

Philip Zimbardo relates the amusing story of Nunzi, a shoemaker and an Italian immigrant.[5] Every day after school a gang of young, American boys came to his shop to taunt and to tease. After attempting in a variety of ways to get the boys to stop, Nunzi hit upon the following solution.

When they arrived the next day after school, he was in front of his store waving a fistful of dollar bills. "Don't ask me why," said Nunzi, "but I'll give each of you a new dollar bill if you will shout at the top of your lungs ten times: 'Nunzi is a dirty Italian swine.' " Taking the money, the boys shouted the chants in unison. The next afternoon Nunzi successfully enticed the gang to repeat their taunts for a mere half dollar. On the third day, however, he stood with a handful of dimes: "Business has not been good and I can only give you each ten cents to repeat your marvelous performance of yesterday."

"You must be crazy," said the ringleader, "to think we would knock ourselves out screaming and cursing for a lousy dime."

"Yah," said another. "We got better things to do with our time than to do favors for dumb Guineas for only a dime." And away the boys went, never to bother Nunzi again.

Do rewards undermine motivation in adults as well? Many studies now show this to be so. In one experiment college students worked on an interesting puzzle for an hour.[6] Half of the subjects were paid a dollar for each of four puzzle solutions they correctly produced; the other half did the same puzzle for no pay. Later all the students were left in a free-choice situation where they could work on other puzzle solutions, read magazines or do anything else they pleased. Those who had been rewarded for solutions showed less interest in working the new puzzles. Rewards had again turned the play into work. Extrinsic rewards undermined intrinsic motivation.

Similarly, adults who were paid to lose weight lost pounds faster than those not paid. But when payments stopped, the former subjects regained some of the lost weight while the latter continued to lose. Research indicates that rewards can even cast a pall over romantic love. Dating couples were asked to think of either the extrinsic rewards (for example, "she/he knows a lot of people") or the intrinsic rewards (for example, "we always have a good time together") they obtained from going out with their partners.[7] When later asked to state their feelings, the couples who had thought about the extrinsic rewards evaluated themselves as being less in love than did those who had thought about intrinsic rewards.

Not all psychologists agree on how these findings should be explained. One interpretation, as I have suggested, is that extrinsic rewards lead people to view an activity differently. They convey to people that the activity does not deserve doing in its own right. Why else would someone offer rewards? People therefore come to see the activity as a means rather than an end, and their actions come under the control of the extrinsic reward. They begin unconsciously to ask, "Is this reward enough to make me want to do 'the work'?" The action, project or whatever is not even considered for itself. If the reward is eventually withdrawn, they judge the activity no longer worth doing.

Does this research on the hidden costs of rewards mean we should never use rewards in our homes, schools or churches? Certainly not. But the findings do suggest we carefully examine how they are used.

How Should We Use Rewards?

Without question, extrinsic rewards motivate people while they are applied. So if we are trying to influence a person to engage in some activity on a short-term basis, the reward route may be the best one to travel. Or if we are convinced the activity will always be inherently boring and distasteful yet has to be performed, rewards may provide the only route. But if we are concerned about fostering intrinsic motivation, if we want our children "taught to live in such a way as to carry out their responsibilities to God and find joy and delight in so doing," then we will use rewards cautiously in our education and evangelism programs.[8] And we will certainly avoid them where they aren't necessary.

What effect do the frequent appeals to personal need and

the ready use of rewards in presenting the gospel have on its credibility? Does the emphasis on comfort before challenge interfere with rather than facilitate others' coming to the truth? Does it in effect say that the Christian lifestyle has little worth or merit in itself? In offering children prizes to get them to memorize Scripture, we might be communicating the message "Really there's nothing in that book worth knowing for its own sake."

Edward Deci suggests, however, that extrinsic rewards do not always undermine intrinsic motivation.[9] In certain cases they may actually *increase* it. Deci claims that every reward —whether money, praise, gold stars or candy bars—has two aspects: a controlling aspect and an informational aspect. The controlling aspect is what satisfies the need and develops the link between the behavior and the reward. In contrast, the informational aspect of a reward conveys to people how well they are doing in meeting the challenge of a particular task. According to Deci, the effect rewards have on people depends on which aspect is the more conspicuous. If the controlling aspect is more obvious, the person is less likely to be intrinsically motivated. But if the informational aspect is salient, intrinsic motivation may actually be enhanced.

What determines whether the controlling or informational aspect of a reward will be more obvious? In part, it's how they are presented. In one study children were offered prizes for playing with a drum.[10] For one group the prize was in plain view. For the other group the prize was absent, and the leaders made no further mention of it during performance. Only the obvious reward produced a significant decrease in intrinsic motivation. Evidently a clearly imaged reward siphons attention away from what becomes the means of getting it.

Anticipated rewards seem to have more serious (and negative) consequences than unanticipated rewards. People are more likely to see the latter as giving them information about their good performance; after all, no attempt was made to bribe them. Rather than emphasizing rewards from the outset to control a class, perhaps teachers might better use them occasionally as an unexpected bonus.

Deci reports that teacher characteristics also have an impact on children's intrinsic motivation.[11] Those who valued order and control in the classroom tended to use rewards as sanctions. Those who favored autonomy, encouraging kids to take responsibility for their own actions, tended to use rewards informationally. The former undermined intrinsic motivation while the latter actually fostered it.

Our View of God's Call

Christian ministers, teachers and missionaries all have their own styles of presenting the Christian message. One thing that significantly shapes their presentations, however, is how they view the nature of God's call. Some seem to view the commands of Scripture as though God had arbitrarily conceived them and then decided to enforce them through reward and punishment. For others the commands come from a loving God whose requirements for our lives are consistent with the way he has created us and with what is best for us. I follow the latter view.

In telling us how we ought to live, God is at the same time telling us how he made us. He informs us of what constitutes the whole person. His prescriptions are really descriptions of what it means to be a complete, fulfilled human being. The point Christians who so eagerly seek God's favor have missed is that the most significant blessings he gives in this life are inherent in obedience itself. They are not granted simply as a consequence of it. In calling us to be more than mere listeners of the Word but doers also, James writes, "The man who looks intently into the perfect law that gives freedom, and continues to do this, not forgetting what he has heard, but doing it—he will be blessed in what he does" (Jas 1:25 NIV).

Probably no story in the New Testament better demonstrates our tendency to miss the blessings that are intrinsic to obedient lives than the familiar parable of the prodigal son. We sympathize with the response of the older brother who objects to the party his father is throwing for the son who was lost but has now returned. Like this older brother, we fail to see the good news that salvation and all its benefits are *now* and are part of living in a right relationship to God our Father.

Self-centered religion misses the central call of Scripture to worship God. It fails to recognize that God has the right to expect our obedience and that he has this right simply because he is God—apart from his capacity to deliver favors or punishments. Ironically, self-centered faith not only misses God's truth, but it also misses his richest blessings. As we noted in chapter three, the refreshing gospel promise is that Christ frees us from self-obsession, frees us to find contentment and peace. Those who come to Christ for the reward will miss the best "reward" that is inherent in the relationship itself.

One of the paradoxes of the Christian life is that the good things God grants come not by deliberately seeking them but as a by-product of turning our lives over to him. While ultimately the Christian life brings fulfillment, that cannot be the goal. To the degree fulfillment is made our goal, it will be lost. God made people to serve him. Only when our commitment, loyalty and allegiance are to him do we come to know what it means to be fully human. It is a by-product of self-transcendence. Christ makes it clear: "For whoever wants to save his life will lose it, but whoever loses his life for me and for the gospel will save it" (Mk 8:35 NIV).

These words show us how false it is to distinguish between Jesus Christ as Savior and as Lord. Yet, rather strangely, it is a distinction that we in the Christian community continue to make. We think a life of obedience is optional for those who are saved. Yet Jesus' words are clear. His being Lord and

Savior are a unity. They come together, or not at all. "For whoever seeks extrinsic rewards will lose intrinsic joy, but whoever relinquishes the self-serving quest in order to serve me will find true fulfillment."

8
Conformity: A Way Out

IN ONE OF THE segments from the television program "Candid Camera," an unsuspecting person waits in an office building for an elevator. The elevator arrives, the doors open, and the passenger steps in. One by one others follow but then proceed to behave strangely: they all face the back. The victim peers quizzically at each, fidgets nervously, and then meekly conforms.

The Impact of Others
While the two previous chapters dealt with our attempts to influence others, these next two are concerned with how we ourselves are influenced. Although we like to think of ourselves as independent, other people's influence is difficult to resist. It often shapes our thoughts, our actions, our

choices. Some of the classical experiments in social psychology have verified its power. What others tell us to do or even how they act sometimes affects our behavior more than does our own perception of what is right.

Imagine you have volunteered to participate in an experiment on visual judgment. You and seven other participants are seated in front of two cards on which are lines of varying lengths. Your task is to judge which of three lines is closest in length to a fourth, which serves as the standard. It is clear to you that line B is the correct answer. But the first person to make a judgment looks carefully at the lines and says, "Line A." To your surprise, so does the second, the third and so on down the line. When your turn finally comes, what will you say? Will you agree with the majority, or will you exercise critical judgment and state what you believe is right?

Asked to predict their own reaction, most people say they will resist influence and report what they know is right. That's what Peter thought, too, before denying Jesus. However, the results of the study indicate otherwise. They demonstrate the powerful effects of an incorrect majority on subjects' responses. Only a quarter of the subjects were able to resist the false norm consistently.[1]

Why do we conform to those around us? One reason is our need to gain others' approval, or to avoid their disapproval. For example, some of those who went along with the group in judging the line lengths did so to avoid appearing different or deviant. They feared being rejected.

Violating social expectations or constraints can be traumatic. Stanley Milgram offers a challenge to those who think it's easy. "Get on a bus," he says, "and sing out loud. Full-throated song now, no humming." While many think it can be readily done, not one in a hundred is able to do it. Or another of Milgram's challenges, one he himself tried, is to board the subway and ask a stranger for his seat.[2] After several attempts in which the words lodged in his throat, Milgram finally choked out the request. Experiencing a moment of panic, he found the man actually giving up his seat. After taking his place, Milgram reported he had an overwhelming need to behave in a way that justified the request. He writes, "I actually felt as if I were going to perish." Only after he was off the train did the tension disappear.

All of us can recite examples from our own lives. Others' pressure, real or imagined, overwhelms us, and we act differently than we would if we were alone, even in ways that violate our Christian conscience. How difficult not to join in approval of that humorous story that disparages another ethnic group or the other sex. And when our children come with their requests that reflect the latest fad at school or on the block, we can give in to their desires; acquiescence is easier than denial, even when it conflicts with what we know should be the answer.

Ten years ago our home was situated in the middle of an old apple orchard. Today we have many close neighbors. While for me the expenditure necessary to maintain a watered and weed-free lawn is at best questionable, I'm sensitive to neighborhood pressure—usually implicit, occasionally explicit—to do something about the one weed-haven on the block. On occasion new students recount the difficulty they are having adjusting to college and particularly to living in the campus residence halls. They've found their lifestyle different from that of other students. And they are uneasy as they see themselves conforming when they know they should resist.

Rejection is painful. To obey God rather than people can be agonizing. We may believe that God's approval has first priority. We may even be convinced that we will withstand tempting influences. Still, the task of being in and not of this world is extraordinarily difficult. When the chips are down, when we have little time or opportunity to reflect on our choice of action, when God seems distant and the pressure is present, we flow with the crowd. With Peter we say by our actions that we "don't know the man."

Milgram's Studies of Obedience

To what degree can social pressure lead us to violate our moral standards? Is it possible that someone can induce us to engage in harmful, destructive acts? Milgram tried to answer this question in what have become the most famous studies in social psychology.[3]

As mentioned in chapter two, men from diverse backgrounds and occupations were recruited to participate in an experiment said to investigate the effects of punishment on learning. The participant was assigned the role of teacher. His task was to deliver an electric shock to the "student" whenever a mistake was made on a simple learning task. The switches on the shock generator ranged from a mild 15 volts to a supposedly dangerous 450 volts. The experimenter instructed the teacher to begin punishment of initial errors with the mild shock and to raise the voltage each time an additional error was made until the highest voltage was being administered. The "student" was an accomplice of the experimenter who, although he received no shock, had been carefully coached to act as though he did. When the student made many mistakes and loudly protested the shocks, the experimenter told the teacher to continue raising the voltage. How far did subjects go? When Milgram described the experiment to psychiatrists, college students and middle-class adults, virtually no one expected anyone to proceed to the end. The psychiatrists guessed one in a thousand. Contrary to expectation, almost two-thirds of the participants fully obeyed, delivering the greatest possible shock.

How could subjects bring themselves to continue shocking the victim? Were they evil people? No, they were not unusually hostile or vicious people. Many belonged to Christian churches and, when asked, firmly stated their moral opposition to injuring others.

Some participants were totally convinced of the wrongness of what they were doing. Yet they succumbed to social pressure. They were afraid that if they broke off they would appear arrogant, discourteous or impolite. One participant, obviously concerned over the welfare of the learner, said to the experimenter, "I don't mean to be rude, sir, but don't you think you should look in on him?" Even the minority who refused to comply in the Milgram study did not reprimand the experimenter for his evil instruction.

John Sabini and Maury Silver have noted the difficulty most of us have in resisting wrongdoing.[4] To question another's behavior openly is crude, uncivil. Even when our rights are violated we are reluctant to object. Better to suffer through the annoying cigarette smoke than to confront the passenger in the seat beside you. And going to the library is less painful than reminding a suitemate to observe quiet hours. Intervening on behalf of another is even more difficult. Who wants to be a meddler? As I left the grocery store last Saturday morning an advocate of children's rights was distributing leaflets. Apparently an advertising campaign is even necessary to get people to report child abuse. Adolph Eichmann stated that the most potent factor in soothing his own conscience was that no one dissented against the Final Solution.

Were Milgram's subjects merely unwilling participants coerced against their better judgment to do evil? Hardly. To view them so is to overlook other important lessons of the study. More subtle forces were also at work.

The Need for Information
Conformity sometimes stems not from our wanting people to like or admire us, but rather from our need to understand ourselves and make sense out of the world. One line of thinking is this: Others, particularly those we respect, may know something we do not know; hence they may provide us with evidence about reality, even about ourselves. By believing and acting as others do, we may gain the benefit of their knowledge.

Another "Candid Camera" clipping provides an amusing

example of this "informational" conformity. Three "Candid Camera" art critics (actually actors) assess the aesthetic merit of an abstract painting. Their enthusiastic evaluations are lengthy and involved, and even include identification of hypothetical objects in the painting. Outside observers are impressed. They agree with these experts. Suddenly one of the experts notices that they have the wrong painting. Quickly the critics reverse their opinion. And so do the onlookers.

This informational influence is different from conformity produced by blatant pressure. Here there is not simply a temporary behavior change in violation of our beliefs. Change is more pervasive, more lasting. The presence of others shapes our inner perspectives, our opinions. And because informational influence generates so little conflict, and may in fact even reduce tension, we are less conscious of it.

Milgram argues that in general people have a strong tendency to accept definitions of reality provided by legitimate authority. Thus in his study we should not view the relationship between the experimenter and subject as one in which a coercive figure merely forces actions from an unwilling subordinate. Rather a legitimate authority redefines the meaning of the situation and the subject accepts it. You are no longer delivering a painful shock; rather you are assisting in the lofty pursuit of scientific knowledge.

Not only do authorities shape our perception of reality. Muzafer Sherif's studies using the "autokinetic phenomenon" show how peers may define for us an ambiguous situation.[5] The phenomenon is produced by projecting a still spot of light on the wall in a dark room. After a few moments, an illusion occurs: the light seems to move. How far does it move? Estimates vary greatly.

In Sherif's study several subjects were taken into a darkened room and asked to estimate how far the light moved. While initial judgments varied considerably, after a while their estimates converged. Influenced by each other, they typically developed a common false belief. But each was unaware that his interpretation of reality was being shaped by the people around him. Social influence extends far beyond our yielding against our better judgment. Others can shape the judgment itself.

Are we Christians as sensitive as we should be to informational conformity? To whom do we look for answers to basic questions? Where do our standards come from—from Scripture, the church or simply the society in which we live? Paul's counsel "Do not be conformed to this world" warns against subtle social influences that alter our perspective and commitment. The world's pervasive influence is recognized by Paul in his command "Be transformed" (Rom 12:2 RSV). Clearly he sees the problem of conformity to this world as extending beyond relatively insignificant beliefs and actions to the core of our being, to our perceptions of reality, our most central beliefs and values. Otherwise the familiar warning against conformity would not be followed with a call for transformation, for a change relating to the entire person.

John Alexander writes, "From our perspective we need only moderate change. Our way of life is only tilted a little to one side. . . . I suggest that Jesus came to tell us things that are not obvious and that he offered a worldview that is quite contrary to the worldview of our culture."[6] In *The Upside-Down Kingdom*, Donald Kraybill argues that the kingdom of God is inverted when compared with the generally accepted values of American society. He writes, "Following Jesus means not only a turning around in some personal habits and attitudes, but most fundamentally it means a completely new way of thinking—a new logic. To follow Jesus means a complete upsetting of the assumptions, logic, values, and presuppositions of the dominant culture."[7] Thus the Christian's mindset changes when informed by Scripture. Definitions of success are inverted as self-sacrifice replaces self-seeking, compassion supplants ambition, sharing overcomes consumption, enemies are loved not hated and status hierarchies are flattened.

What's a Christian to Do?

The conformity research has implications for Christian lifestyle. Most fundamentally this social psychological literature questions our individualism, our refusal to recognize that we are interdependent and that we do influence each other. The illusion of independence pervades the church. We not only underestimate the problem of conformity to this world, but when we do recognize it our attempt to deal with it is often misguided. We think the solution is found in developing greater independence; we teach our children, "Dare to be a Daniel; dare to stand alone."

Living as Christians is necessarily a community task. It requires social support. Without a sustaining environment it is hard to develop and even more difficult to maintain a Christian lifestyle. Being created social means that we need to be nourished; we must be encouraged by each other to live our commitments. It's tough to maintain one's Amish identity while living alone in San Francisco.

Social influence is not inherently evil. Without doubt our actions are shaped by the people around us. But this very fact that can work against a Christian lifestyle can also work to enhance it. Consider a variation of the Milgram obedience study: Three teachers, rather than one, were assigned the task of punishing the learner. Two of the three teachers were confederates who had been told to disobey the experimenter after the learner's first vehement protest. In this situation, the obedience of the remaining teacher usually dropped dramatically. From the compliant two-thirds in the original study it fell to 10 per cent. Milgram concluded that "the mutual support provided by men for each other is the strongest bulwark we have against the excesses of authority.[8] Ironically, the majority of defiant subjects denied that the confederate teachers' action was the critical factor in their own defiance. This again illustrates that we are often unaware of others' influence.

Other studies have produced similar findings when the unanimity of the group is broken by having one member give a dissenting view. People provided with a single ally, a partner, show much more allegiance to truth than those who stand alone against the group. Hence disciples sent out two by two are provided mutual support in challenging the existing social order.

Observations of small groups, together with recent laboratory experiments, also indicate that when like-minded people interact, their initial tendencies intensify. For example, as members of diet groups discuss their mutual problem, their shared desire to cut their food consumption may heighten the commitment of each. In one laboratory study separate groups composed of relatively prejudiced or unprejudiced students were asked to respond—both before and after discussion—to issues involving racial attitudes, such as property rights versus open housing. Discussion among like-minded students increased the initial gap between the two groups. Each group became stronger in its own convictions.[9]

Christian fellowship can heighten spiritual identity, especially when members concentrate their interaction among themselves. As Thomas à Kempis recognized long ago, "a devout communing on spiritual things sometimes greatly helps the health of the soul especially when men of one mind and spirit meet and speak and commune together." Peter and Paul, freed from jail, met with their fellow believers and then went out to preach with even greater boldness. The chief dynamic of John Wesley's Methodist movement was the weekly small group meeting. Those who heard the powerful preaching but did not experience the support of the group sooner or later reverted to their former ways.

The Importance of Christian Community

If people are to live distinctively Christian lives, the spirit of individualism must be overcome. Loyalty to Christ is next to impossible without a relationship to his body, to a fellowship of Christians who contribute to each other's upbuilding. Although time and again we are reminded that the New Testament church was a believing community, we have lost this perspective. As Andrew Kuyvenhoven has observed, "Many of us become positively uneasy when we are made to realize that God wants us to contribute to the 'upbuilding' of others —by word and deed. It is certainly a lot easier to 'attend church' than to 'be church.' "[10] Arthur Gish puts it even more strongly: "The church should not accept confessions of faith and commitments without providing nurture and support to help people keep their promises. We fail people by not supporting and helping them keep their commitments."[11]

The fellowship of believers is necessary, however, not only for the support it provides, but also for defining what Christian commitment means in terms of everyday living. Jim Wallis suggests that Christians have often made their stand against culture in the wrong places. "Twentieth century evangelicals," he writes, "have largely ignored the most basic conflicts between the gospel and the American culture while carefully clinging to carefully defined separations from the world over trivial matters of personal behavior."[12] Richard Foster has argued that one of the great tasks confronting the Christian is not "Do I conform or not?" but "Which issues demand nonconformity and which issues do not?"[13]

Defining a Christian pattern of living is difficult and is necessarily a community task. We need each other. And while the identification of general principles will be important, more than this is needed. Even after we have absorbed the general rules we stumble over their application.

For example, a group may identify resisting materialism as a general goal, but what does that mean in terms of lifestyle? Perhaps, as Hendrik Hart and Ron Sider have suggested, we learn to practice community by dealing with spe-

cific issues and by starting in small ways. Within the church
a few families who know they are spending too much might
meet together to make changes in the way they live. They
can discuss family finances and evaluate family budgets.
Expenditures for houses, cars and vacations can be discussed
honestly in terms of individual needs and the needs of God's
kingdom. Tips for simpler living can be shared. And when
decisions are reached, the people in the small community
can encourage, support and pray for one another.

Separate groups might form to address other issues or
problems. Those who are horrified at racism or concerned
about the threat of nuclear holocaust might consider practical ways they could implement their Christian confession.
Such groups need not become cliques nor judgmental of
those in the larger Christian community. To combat that
possibility, Hart suggests that the small communities remain
open and that from time to time families change projects.

So, in taking seriously Paul's call for nonconformity, let's
realize that neither anticonformity nor independence is
the goal. Rather, as a community we seek a new conformity
and another influence, that of Jesus Christ. In his letter
to the Philippians, Paul makes it clear: "Being in full accord and of one mind, . . . have this mind among yourselves,
which is yours in Christ Jesus" (Phil 2:2, 5 RSV). This will
happen only as we seek the Lord together.

9
When Groupthink Strikes

THE COUNCIL OF A SMALL but rapidly growing church discusses plans to construct an elaborate, new facility. The meetings spent reviewing plans are free of disagreement. Although one council member, a middle-aged real-estate broker, has some private doubts about the church's ability to finance the project, he hesitates to puncture the group's enthusiasm. When he did voice his reservation over lunch with another council member, he was told, "You lack faith." Inspired by its youthful, dynamic pastor and certain the new building will both attract new members and enable a host of new programs, the council unanimously votes to proceed. Bonds are sold, a sizable bank loan secured. Yet just eighteen months later the same council members find it impossible to meet even the interest payments on their loan. Disaster looms. The council members wonder how they so easily reached the decision they did.

How could such a fiasco occur? A single individual's judgment might be clouded, but can an entire group be blind? Doesn't group discussion sharpen perspectives, promote reflection, ensure better judgment? In chapter eight we argued that we need others not only for social support but for help in defining a Christian pattern of living, especially in the face of worldly pressures. When we combine the knowledge and talents of many, we should reach better solutions. But groups do not always have favorable consequences for their members. What if the Christian community we are in is wrong on an important issue? How can we avoid conformity to a mistaken view within the church? That is the issue of this chapter.

C. S. Lewis's Screwtape recognized that a small group of like-minded people, isolated from outside contact, may turn in on itself and become self-serving and narrow in perspective. He writes the junior devil, Wormwood, "We want the Church to be small not only that fewer men may know the Enemy but also that those who do may acquire the uneasy intensity and the defensive self-righteousness of a secret society or a clique."[1]

Irving Janis provides a fascinating analysis of how group influence may have such effects.[2] Janis examined the group dynamics underlying the Vietnam war, the Bay of Pigs invasion, our failure to be prepared for the attack on Pearl Harbor, and the invasion of North Korea. He argues that the policy-making groups responsible for the fiascoes suffered from groupthink. The desire to maintain group harmony had led to a suppression of dissent. Critical judgment, independent analytical thought and the weighing of pros and cons were subverted in an attempt to maintain consensus in the group. Before examining groupthink in the church, let's look at the dynamics of groupthink in general.

Groupthink: A Case Study

In the Kennedy administration's decision to invade Cuba's Bay of Pigs, Janis identifies both the major causes and symptoms of groupthink. Perhaps the most important cause is group cohesiveness. Kennedy's inner circle enjoyed a strong esprit de corps; the members prized their membership in the group and felt strongly committed to it. To maintain these good group feelings, they suppressed disagreeable thoughts. This cohesiveness was accompanied by isolation from outside contact; alternative viewpoints critical of the group's plans to invade Cuba were simply not discussed. Moreover, Kennedy was a highly directive leader who early in the group's deliberations had indicated his approval of the plan to invade. Finally, no procedures had been established for generating and exploring alternatives to the invasion plan.

These conditions fostered a concurrence-seeking tendency and produced the symptoms of groupthink. The high morale fostered an illusion of invulnerability which led the group to take risks that its members as individuals would not have considered. A second symptom of groupthink manifested by the Kennedy team was a shared illusion of unanimity. The group meetings in which the basic features of the invasion plan won approval were relatively free of disagreement. Arthur Schlesinger Jr. later reflected, "Our meetings took place in a curious atmosphere of assumed consensus. Had one senior advisor opposed the adventure, I believe that Kennedy would have cancelled it. No one spoke against it."[3] The unanimity, however, was not real. Conflict was just beneath the surface, camouflaged by members' reluctance to reveal their private reservations.

What had created this feeling of unanimity? Janis saw it coming from the self-censorship of each person and what he calls "mind-guards." The more difficult and ambiguous the situation, the more each individual relies on the judgment of other group members to define reality and the appropriate course of action. And when a group of persons who respect each other's judgment arrives at a unanimous view, each member is likely to feel the belief must be true. Victims of groupthink keep quiet about their doubts.

Self-appointed mind-guards reproach potential deviants. At a large birthday party for his wife, Attorney General Robert F. Kennedy took Schlesinger aside and asked him why he was opposed. Kennedy listened and finally said, "You may be right or you may be wrong, but the President has made up his mind. Don't push it any further."[4]

Social pressures to conform were also placed on group members by the leader, President Kennedy. CIA representatives, who strongly supported the invasion plan, were called to refute any critic. Schlesinger states that his guilt feelings for not raising objections within the group meetings "were tempered by the knowledge that a course of objection would have accomplished little save to gain me a name as a nuisance."[5] To disagree would have evoked disapproval from the leader as well as from other group members.

The belief of the group in its own inherent morality coupled with the shared stereotypes of Castro as weak, evil and stupid further justified the decision to proceed. Group members rationalized away warning signs of potential disaster. The decision was confirmed: a small band of Cuban exiles secretly landed on a beachhead with the aim of overthrowing the government of Fidel Castro. The result was a rout. Within three days the ragtag band had been overwhelmed and its secret mission traced directly to the U.S. government. It was the "perfect failure," and John F. Kennedy asked, "How could I have been so stupid to let them go ahead?"[6]

Groupthink in the Church: Some Underlying Causes
Janis limits his study of groupthink to small decision-making bodies in government and business. His analysis, however, has obvious application to any area where cohesive groups make decisions. Are the conditions which promote group-

think present in the church?

Several factors in the church may make it susceptible. To the degree we are sensitive to the destructive effects of conforming to the larger society, some church people may want to isolate themselves from outside contact. Attacks on the church from outside, if there have been any, may contribute to cohesiveness within—a sense of "us" against "them"—and make church unity an end in itself. We reason that only a united church can defend itself against those attacks, survive and grow. We believe that only a church free of conflict can provide a strong and vital witness to the world. We view even quiet dissent and disagreement as disruptive, and open conflict as destructive, as though it might shake stability and endanger the very existence of the church. Ironically, in our press for unity within the church, we may lose the very strength and vitality we seek—the vigor that healthy and loving conflict can bring.

Unthinking compliance in the church may therefore have its basis not in apathy or laziness, but in fear of conflict. The problem is that in our desire for consensus we easily fall into blind conformity. We do not openly examine doubts about whether present doctrine and practice are consistent with the Word of God. Unfortunately, our reluctance to question existing beliefs and practices may lead to unwarranted assumptions. An early field study of a small rural community, Elm Hollow, illustrates what may happen.[7]

Elm Hollow residents were almost unanimous in saying they disapproved of playing cards, drinking liquor and smoking ciragettes. However, many members were more than willing to play cards, drink hard cider and smoke, as long as it was done behind closed doors. But each resident was firmly convinced that the others were against doing these things. Then the new pastor began to play cards in public. The people discovered they had made unwarranted assumptions about each others' attitudes, and the hypocrisy ended. The "existing beliefs" had never existed at all!

Whenever we accept the apparent status quo, we basically fail to articulate our own opinion. And *Christian* response to the important social issues of our day is much needed. The church too often seems to follow rather than lead in significant matters like racial injustice, women's rights and the nuclear arms race. In my experience at church-related colleges, I have observed students accepting without question what is presented in the classroom. They are reluctant to question, to challenge, to voice dissent. And when students do not examine critically what is taught by the light of Scripture, they likely fail as well to integrate their learning into their world view and lifestyle. What they say and how they live can be as separate as "belief" and action in Elm Hollow. Generally speaking, the church will always fail where it is not self-critical, where it fails to hold up its teachings and practices to honest study and critical examination under the Word. It is just as necessary for the group as it is for the individual.

Another factor which may contribute to groupthink in the church is the false idea that faith is antagonistic to exercising critical judgment on any issue. This distorted perspective implies that the rational analysis of a problem, a careful search for information and independent analytical thinking may well be proper for solving problems in government, business and education, but they are not appropriate for resolving issues within the church; in fact, such analysis is diametrically opposed to trusting God. In one recent church meeting the council recommended to the full membership the construction of a new educational complex. One concerned individual asked, "Have you surveyed the congregation to determine its ability and willingness to meet the expense?" Before either the council or pastor could respond, one member suggested that such a survey was not only unnecessary but would reflect a failure to trust God's care and willingness to bless the work of the church.

We are indeed dependent on God. But such a recognition

must never lead us to neglect our responsibility to pursue knowledge of God's will through every available means. To fail to exercise the capacities he has given us to learn his will for our lives is to ignore one of the major ways through which his Spirit works. The rational analysis of a problem, the exercise of critical judgment and the pursuit of knowledge through every legitimate means are in keeping with the recognition of our dependence on God. They are all quite consistent with the fervent prayer that God may guide us in arriving at decisions that conform to his will.

Symptoms of Groupthink

We don't encourage loyalty to God by a faith that refuses to exercise critical judgment. Such refusal readily leads to groupthink. Our own initial ideas or impulses become identified with God's will, and we create an illusion of invulnerability and a belief in our own inherent morality. Alternatives are either not examined or quickly dismissed. Any suggestions to review or reconsider, to delay temporarily or exercise caution are rationalized as reflecting a lack of faith.

The conformity pressures that Janis found within the small decision-making bodies in government also operate to ensure consensus in the church. Self-appointed mindguards frequently seek to silence any individual who breaks the complacency surrounding current teaching or practice. The threat of ostracism may be used to keep the potential deviant in line. It may be the leaders within the church who experience those pressures most acutely. As Janis indicates in his analysis of group decision making, those in positions of leadership are in no way immune to social pressure. When a theologian questions a teaching or practice within the church, the call to the heresy hunt often sounds. We demand unquestioning compliance of our theologians and threaten severe penalties for failure to yield obedience. Perhaps we should examine whether we place undue pressure on our leaders, pressures that may contribute to groupthink.

Of course, leaders may also exert strong social pressures on the membership in an effort to maintain consensus within the church. Moreover, the scriptural teaching that office bearers have been chosen by God can be readily distorted. Human words can easily become equated with the Word of God, creating a powerful deterrent to debate or disagreement with those in positions of leadership. Questions concerning correct Christian belief and action will not be raised, and we should therefore not be surprised to find in the church, as in Elm Hollow, frequent inconsistencies between the public and the private spheres of behavior and belief.

More subtle social pressures may also operate in the Christian community to ensure unanimity. As we saw earlier, developing a Christian perspective on life is a difficult and often ambiguous task. We struggle to discover how God's Word speaks to specific issues confronting local churches and to learn God's will for our daily lives. These are all community tasks; we look to each other for assistance in sorting out the proper answers to these questions.

We should be aware, however, that given our concurrence-seeking tendency this high reliance on consensual valida-tion can easily result in self-censorship. Personal doubts, misgivings and questions about generally accepted teaching and practice seldom find expression. Others' silence is assumed to mean their full accord. The greater respect we have for each other and for church leaders, the more likely we will keep silent about our misgivings and minimize our doubts. In resolving controversy, we will appeal to past teachings and credal statements rather than taking a fresh, new look at Scripture. Thus the church may stagnate in either its understanding or application of God's Word.

The more difficult and ambiguous the task, the more likely we are to adhere to the established norm and to engage in self-censorship. Once the illusion of unanimity is shattered, however, we can no longer feel complacently self-confident about the old answers. Each person must then face the annoying realization that there are, in fact, troublesome uncertainties and unresolved issues.

Likewise, the more amiability and esprit de corps there is within the group, the greater the danger that critical thinking will be replaced by groupthink. Ironically, those groups that appear to be the most vigorous may also be the most subject to groupthink. To the degree that important social needs are met, a clublike atmosphere may pre-empt concern for the difficult tasks that must be faced. The fact that many of us within the church work together, worship together and socialize together may suppress critical thought. The result may be a failure to offer direction and leadership in confronting the critical issues of the day.

No one would deny, of course, that for any community to exist its members must agree on certain basic norms. The church has that in its shared commitment to God's Word as the foundation for its very existence. Having clearly identified our common commitment, however, we should be open to discussion and debate. We should realize that conflict within the church can be constructive, that through it the church can grow, become stronger and better promote the coming of God's kingdom. When disagreements are aired openly rather than allowed to smolder, new understandings can develop and relationships may be healed. The unity we share in Jesus Christ does not prevent but in fact *provides* the basis for constructive disagreement and debate within the church.

Preventing Groupthink

Janis not only identified the causes and chief symptoms of groupthink; he also proposed some techniques for preventing it. His suggestions attempt to generate constructive conflict within a group. While they apply most directly to the small decision-making group, we will see that, in certain cases, the application can be readily extended to the church.

First, Janis suggests, the leader of the group should assign the role of critical evaluator to each member. That is, the leader should encourage members to voice objections and express doubts about the ideas and plans presented. The exercise of independent thought and judgment should be held in high regard rather than discouraged. It is probably important that the leader make this norm explicit from the outset, and not assume group members will naturally follow it. All of this means, of course, that the leader as well as the group as a whole must be willing to consider criticism and be open to change.

The first suggestion for avoiding groupthink has obvious significance for church council and committee meetings. However, it also has application at the broader church level. The church must be open to criticism and be ready to change. Members should be encouraged to express their doubts and concerns about established doctrines and practices of the church. While our unvarying, infallible source of truth is the Word of God, we dare not close the book on its proper interpretation or application. Open discussion, debate and continuous re-evaluation should become the norm rather than the exception. Avenues of communication must be provided which allow for a conflict of ideas, and specific procedures might well be established through which leaders and all people of the church may express dissent with commonly accepted teaching. Only in this way will the church progress in its understanding of difficult doctrinal issues as well as in providing answers to the critical problems facing our society and world. Willingness to change is openness to the Spirit.

A second suggestion which Janis makes for avoiding groupthink is that the group divide into subgroups to meet separately under different chairpersons and then come back together to hammer out differences. Subgrouping reduces the chances that the larger group will reach an immediate consensus by not recognizing its own faulty underlying assumptions. When the church is considering or formulating recommendations on any major issue, such as new evangelism or building programs at the local level or specific doctrinal or social issues at the institutional level, the work is often assigned to committees. To avoid groupthink, Janis suggests that more than one committee or subcommittee meet under different leadership to reach initial agreement on the same issue. After this has been done, subgroups can re-form into one group to reach a final decision.

Third, Janis argues that one or more outside experts be invited in, not only to present information but also to challenge, if they wish, the existing ideas of group members. My own experience on church committees suggests that we rarely implement this procedure. Perhaps respect for the autonomy of individual congregations explains why a local church committee rarely calls on the resources or judgment of neighboring churches in reaching major program or policy decisions. This seems to be the case even when those decisions may have implications for all churches in the community. Similarly, while most church councils and committees seek to maintain an "open door" policy, they are in fact often isolated and removed from the membership of their own church. Church leaders should not expect that most members will actively seek them out to voice questions or objections, nor should they assume that silence or failure to appear at committee meetings means assent with existing policy. Rather, leaders and office bearers must often painstakingly seek out the views and questions of the persons they serve.

On a broader level there has been a general tendency on the part of the church to insulate itself from outside critics and to reject the notion that anything useful could be learned from the non-Christian "expert." I recall that as a student member of a college committee I participated in a decision to permit on campus only speakers who shared our common Christian perspective. The decision was hastily arrived at as a result of criticism directed at the school for inviting a speaker who proved to be highly controversial. On reflection, the decision was a product of groupthink, and it was fortunately reversed within eighteen months. Nevertheless, there still exists within the church a fear that outside critics, if listened to, will destroy us. We fail to recognize that they may have something significant for us to hear.

To avoid groupthink Janis also suggests that leaders initially refrain from stating their position, preference or expectation. This will permit an atmosphere of open inquiry in which a wide range of alternatives may be explored. Authoritarian leaders who state almost at the outset, "It's obvious that this matter can be resolved with little discussion," or, "I would be surprised to find anyone in disagreement with my position," are inviting groupthink. Similarly, leaders within the church sometimes respond almost reflexively to conflict with appeals to maintain "unity in Christ." What is often meant is, "Don't disagree with me or with the majority." Such an approach will hardly promote openness or diversity of viewpoint.

Janis's additional proposals may also prove useful. He suggests, for example, that at every meeting a different group member be assigned the role of devil's advocate, attacking premature consensus and challenging existing ideas. And, whenever it is feasible, a policy-making group should hold a "second chance" meeting before implementing any decision. At this special meeting every member should be encouraged to become the devil's advocate. Everyone should present to the group any objections he or she can think of that have not yet been adequately discussed.

The church was established by God himself, and we as members of the body of Christ must continue to look to the power and leading of his Spirit. I am not suggesting that if Christians simply rely on their own capacity for rational analysis and critical judgment, all will go well. What I am saying is that the church, while divinely instituted, is also a human institution. What applies to other human institutions applies to the church as well. God works through the minds and actions of his people to accomplish his purposes. As God's agents, we have the responsibility to apply fully the abilities he gives both in learning his will for our lives and in furthering his kingdom.

Just as consensus in the church should not become an end in itself, so we should not promote conflict for conflict's sake. We are to be concerned with building a strong and vital church for the ministry of God's kingdom.[8] Sharing some initial consensus is necessary for a group to function or even exist. And reaching agreement on an issue or problem is essential if the group is to be effective.

Sometimes, when resolving trivial issues or when time is of the essence, conflict must be discouraged. There is a difference between conflict that produces growth and conflict which simply delays action or destroys relationships; we must be discerning in this. The solution, however, lies in accepting and regulating conflict, not in eliminating it. Conflict as a regular agent of decision making can free us from the trap of groupthink to provide valid guidance for the church.

Part III
Relating

THE APOSTLE JOHN taught that our relationships to God and to one another are inseparable: "If anyone says, 'I love God,' but keeps on hating his brother, he is a liar; for if he doesn't love his brother who is right there in front of him, how can he love God whom he has never seen?" (1 Jn 4:20 LB). Part I explored social thought, and Part II examined certain aspects of social influence. Social psychology is also concerned with how we relate to one another; so in Part III we consider social relations.

Chapter ten introduces two social psychological principles to explain why it is that yesterday's luxuries have a way of becoming today's necessities, resulting in commiserating "poortalk." Fortunately, these principles also suggest remedies which can enable us to be more satisfied with our affluence and more sensitive to others' poverty.

What attracts us to another person? Chapter eleven shows how the reward principle often leads us into friendship. Christ, however, presents us with a more challenging and inspiring vision of love. He both models and calls us to concern for another's welfare with no expectation of reward.

Jesus' classic illustration of altruism, the parable of the good Samaritan, has provided the impetus for an interesting social psychological experiment. Chapter twelve examines the study's findings, along with other research on our willingness to help others.

Our concern for justice often moves us to help victims of oppression. Chapter thirteen explores how the desire for a just world may foster constructive social change, but may also ironically, serve to perpetuate injustice.

Becoming aware of these tendencies is a necessary first step toward creating Shalom. Chapter fourteen examines the biblical vision of peacemaking. Identifying several sources of human conflict, it suggests some principles of Christian peacemaking.

10
Why Do
the Rich Feel
So Poor?

THE WESTERN INDUSTRIALIZED nations have undergone an astonishing growth in prosperity since World War 2. In the past three decades the average American's disposable income has doubled. But this unprecedented rapid growth in real income may now be ending, say some economic prophets, or at least it ought not be allowed to continue. Skyrocketing energy costs, diminishing supplies of nonrenewable resources and exploding population have brought together an unlikely chorus of conservationists, economists, politicians and scientists who warn that limited growth, zero growth or even economic decline is in store for us.

Even if the doomsday visions do not materialize, we must still cope with our fluctuating economy and its cycles of inflation and recession. Many Americans today think that their economic condition is worsening. We complain to one another that we can no longer afford things we used to buy routinely. When bill-paying time comes, we bemoan the near-impossibility of trying to make ends meet at today's prices. Aware of our economic anguish, a presidential candidate routs the incumbent with a politically astute question: "Are you better off than you were four years ago?"

Ironically, the income data in figure 3 suggest that the average American should have answered Ronald Reagan's question with a yes. Despite all the "poortalk," the fact is that buying power had not diminished. Even if we take into account increased taxes as well as inflation, real disposable income for the average American rose dramatically between 1935 and 1976 and has risen slightly since then.

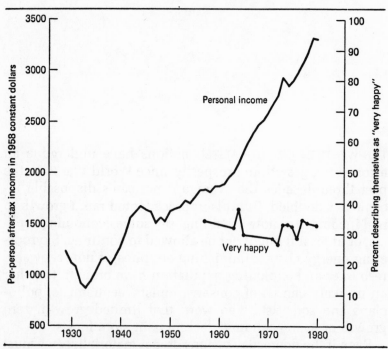

Figure 3.   *Money. Does it buy happiness? (Taken from Social Psychology by D. G. Myers, © 1983. Used by permission of McGraw-Hill Book Co., New York, New York.)*

Why All the Poortalk?

Why then do middle-class Americans not *feel* more affluent? Why do yesterday's luxuries become today's necessities, leading most people to feel that their needs are always slightly greater than their income? And what trauma may we expect if the predicted limits to growth do in fact materialize and we enter a slow-growth or no-growth era?

Several principles from psychological research can help us understand the emotions that accompany economic fluctuations. These concepts assist in explaining our insatiability, and they prompt us to consider alternative routes to personal security and well-being.

The first principle is the *adaptation-level* phenomenon. Although research on this topic is relatively recent, the idea dates back to the Epicurean and Stoic philosophers. The basic point is that we use our past to calibrate our present experience and to form expectations for the future. Success and failure, satisfaction and dissatisfaction, are relative to our prior experience. If our achievements rise above those expectations, we experience success and satisfaction. If our achievements fall below the neutral point defined by prior experience, we feel dissatisfied and frustrated.

Increased material goods, leisure time or social prestige provides an initial surge of pleasure. Yet all too soon the feeling wanes. Black-and-white television, once a thrill, begins to seem ordinary. Then we need something better, a bigger "fix," to give us another surge of pleasure.

This principle was also plainly evident in the high suicide rate among people who lost their wealth during the depression. A temporary infusion of wealth can leave one feeling worse than if it had never come. For this reason, Christmas-basket charity may be counterproductive, making the recipient family more acutely aware of its poverty the other 364 days a year while doing nothing to relieve the impoverished state.

If, however, the improvements persist, we adapt to them.

Our experience is recalibrated so that what was formerly seen as positive is now only neutral and what was formerly neutral becomes negative. Psychologists Philip Brickman and Donald Campbell noted that this principle, well grounded in research, predicts that humanity will never create a social paradise on earth.[1] Once achieved, our utopia would soon be subject to recalibration so that we would again sometimes feel pleasure, sometimes feel deprived and sometimes feel neutral.

This is why, despite the increase in real income during the past several decades, the average American today reports no greater feeling of general happiness and satisfaction than was the case thirty years ago. In 1957, for example, 35 per cent of the population reported themselves "very happy." By 1980, after two decades of growing affluence, how many declared themselves "very happy"? Only 33 per cent. Moreover, surveys in rich and poor nations do not reveal striking differences in self-reported happiness. Egyptians are as happy as West Germans; Cubans are as happy as Americans. "Poverty," said Plato, "consists not in the decrease of one's possessions but in the increase of one's greed." Assuming that inequality of wealth persists, there is a real sense in which we shall "always have the poor." The poor remain poor partly because the criteria for poverty are continually redefined.

A recent study of state lottery winners illustrates the adaptation-level principle.[2] Researchers at Northwestern University found that people felt good about winning the lottery; they typically said that it was one of the best things ever to happen to them. Yet their reported happiness did not increase. In fact, everyday activities like reading or eating breakfast became less pleasurable. It seemed that winning the lottery was such a high point that life's ordinary pleasures paled by comparison.

The dissatisfactions bred by adapting to affluence are compounded when we compare ourselves with others. When climbing the ladder of success, people look up, not down. They pay attention to where they are going, usually neglecting where they have come from. Such upward comparison further whets human appetites. Unfortunately, the ladder's rungs go on forever. So unless we gain a broader perspective we will be forever comparing ourselves with those above us. And doing so inevitably empowers a second principle, *relative deprivation.*

The term *relative deprivation* was coined by researchers studying levels of satisfaction of American World War 2 soldiers. Ironically, those in the Air Corps, where promotions were rapid and widespread, were more frustrated about their rate of promotion than were those in the Military Police, for whom promotions were slow and unpredictable. In retrospect, we realize that the Air Corps promotion rate was rapid and that, according to those principles noted in chapter three, most Air Corps personnel probably perceived themselves as better than the average Air Corps member. It's therefore likely that their aspirations soared higher than their achievements. The result? Frustration!

The self-serving bias can fuel feelings of relative deprivation. When merit salary raises are awarded, at least half the employees will receive only an average raise or less. Since few see themselves as average or below average, many will feel that an injustice has been done. The shortest line of all would be composed of those who feel they were overpaid.

People's impression that they have been unjustly evaluated does not necessarily signify actual injustice. Even if God himself prescribed the salary increases according to his most perfect justice, many would still be upset—unless their self-perceptions distributed themselves in conformity with the true distribution of employee excellence, which they surely would not. A fixed-percentage or fixed-increment salary increase does not resolve the problem. Many people may then feel that equal pay is, for them, inequitable, since they are more competent and committed than most others.

The resentment that accompanies high inflation, even in times when wage increases keep pace with prices, partly reflects the self-serving bias. Economist George Katona observed that people tend to perceive their wage increases as the reward for their talent and effort, and thus they see price increases as cheating them of their rightful gains.

The relative deprivation principle has some intriguing implications. For example, as a family or employee group increases in affluence and social status, it elevates the comparison standards by which it evaluates its own achievements. Paradoxically, this means that actual gains in income, possessions or status may be offset by psychological losses stemming from the change in comparison group. Liberation movements, by raising their adherents' aspirations and expectations, may simultaneously stimulate increases in their actual achievements *and* in their perceived relative deprivation. Becoming a feminist is probably not initially going to alleviate a woman's frustration with her lot in life. In the short run, at least, she is as likely to feel more frustrated.

Psychologists have found no upper bounds for the rising aspirations embodied in this principle. The ladder seems infinite. Unless we renounce the climb, we will be forever comparing ourselves with others above us. We are like rats on a hedonic treadmill, requiring an ever-increasing level of income and social status just to feel "neutral."

How to Be Middle Class and Feel Rich
All this sounds a bit pessimistic. Is there any cause for optimism? We can draw some consolation from the fact that the adaptation-level principle works in both directions: If personal choice or economic pressures drive us to adopt a simpler life, we will eventually adapt and recover life's balance of happiness, discontent and neutrality. In the aftermath of the 1970's gas price hikes, Americans managed to reduce their "need" for large, gas-slurping cars. Even paraplegics, the blind and other severely handicapped people

generally adapt to their situation and eventually recover a normal or near-normal level of life satisfaction.[3] Victims of traumatic accidents would surely exchange places with those of us who are not paralyzed, and most of us would be delighted to win a state lottery. Yet, after a period of adjustment, none of these three groups departs appreciably from the others in moment-to-moment happiness. Human beings have an enormous adaptive capacity.

What more active steps can we take to stay up psychologically even in a down economy? The adaptation-level and relative deprivation principles offer several constructive implications for all, but especially for Christians who wish like Paul to learn "godliness with contentment" (1 Tim 6:6 RSV).

First, *we can use the spectacles of history to cure our economic myopia.* Most of us are chronically preoccupied with the short run—with comparing our profits and salaries with last month's or last year's figures, and agonizing over any ground we have lost. But when we lift our gaze to the more distant past, we see that economic stagnation of the 1980s is but a barely perceptible downward blip on almost five decades of rising affluence. Perhaps taking a longer-run perspective, such as comparing the 1982 recession to the 1930s' depression, can trigger greater satisfaction.

Second, *we can recognize the relativity of happiness.* If we feel deprived, we can first analyze our present life satisfaction in light of the adaptation-level principle, pinpointing recent changes in income or status and evaluating how much effect each has had on our happiness. Most will realize that past fluctuations in income, possessions or social status have had only a transient impact on our satisfaction.

Perhaps that is why the Declaration of Independence specifies as an inalienable right only the *pursuit* of happiness: our elation over an achievement always fades into neutrality, only to be replaced by a new level of striving. Just becoming aware of this fact can be a first step toward gaining mastery over the adaptation-level phenomenon in our lives. Recog-

nizing the relativity of our perceived deprivation can similarly diminish our feelings of actual deprivation. In short,
realizing our past captivity to our appetites can open us to a
new perspective on life, such as Jesus taught in his Sermon
on the Mount: Happy are those who renounce selfish ambition. We will find abundant life by losing our life, not by
clutching at things. Simple living unclutters the heart and
makes room for those things that have ultimate value.

Epictetus, the Stoic philosopher-slave, urged likewise:
"Seek not that the things which happen should happen as
you wish; but wish the things which happen to be as they
are, and you will have a tranquil flow of life." The preacher
of Ecclesiastes expressed a similar sentiment: "I have also
learned why people work so hard to succeed: it is because
they envy the things their neighbors have. But it is useless.
It is like chasing the wind. They say that a man would be a
fool to fold his hands and let himself starve to death. Maybe
so, but it is better to have only a little, with peace of mind,
than be busy all the time with both hands, trying to catch the
wind" (Eccles 4:4-6 TEV). This is not to commend apathy
and fatalism. Epictetus cautioned us to distinguish between
those things that are in our power and those that are not. If
the source of our perceived deprivation is subject to our control, then we should struggle mightily to correct the problem.
If, however, it lies outside our power, we should accept our
situation with calmness and equanimity.

Third, *we can cut the "poortalk,"* that incessant grousing
about how we can't exist on our mere $20,000 incomes. Poor-
talk by relatively affluent people is objectionable on two
counts. First, it is insensitive to the truly impoverished, just
as self-pitying "fat-talk" by a slightly overweight person is
insensitive to the truly obese, or "sick-talk" by a reasonably
healthy person is insensitive to the agonies of those seriously
ill. And, second, poortalk sours our thinking.

Social psychologists have repeatedly observed that what
we say influences what we think and feel. Thus one way for

middle-class folk to gain a healthier perspective on their situation is to cut the poortalk. "I need that," can become, "I want that." "I am underpaid," can become, "I spend more than I make." And that most familiar middle-class statement, "I can't afford it," can become, "I choose to spend my money on other things." This last example acknowledges the fact that most of us could afford almost any reasonable item, if we made it a top priority. The fact is, we have other priorities on which we choose to spend our limited income. The choice is ours. "I can't afford it" denies the choices we have made, reducing us to self-pitying victims.

Fourth, *we can choose our comparison groups intentionally.* We can resist the tendency to measure ourselves against those higher on the ladder of success and choose instead to compare ourselves with those less fortunate. Earlier generations were taught to perform such comparisons by way of "counting one's blessings." We can avoid settings in which we are surrounded by other people's luxury and wealth. We can even go out of our way to confront true poverty, to drown our relative deprivations in the sea of absolute deprivation that exists for so many human beings. Discovering how relatively small our problems are can make us more sensitive to real poverty, enabling us better to see as Jesus sees. We can begin to appreciate the extent to which some people's unmet needs—clean water, adequate nutrition, medical care—are things we take for granted.

Even imagining others' misfortunes may trigger greater life satisfaction. As Abraham Maslow noted, "All you have to do is to go to a hospital and hear all the simple blessings that people never before realized *were* blessings—being able to urinate, to sleep on your side, to be able to swallow, to scratch an itch, etc. Could *exercises* in deprivation educate us faster about all our blessings?"[4] A research team led by Marshall Dermer put a number of University of Wisconsin-Milwaukee women through some imaginative exercises in deprivation.[5] After viewing vivid depictions of how grim life was in Milwaukee in 1900, or after imagining and then writing about various personal tragedies such as being burned and disfigured, the women expressed a greater sense of satisfaction with the quality of their own lives.

Finally, *we can view life from the eternal perspective.* Christian faith encourages us with the good news that our struggles will not endure forever. Authentic Christian hope is not built on a make-believe escape from life's frustrations and agonies, but it does promise that evil, deprivation and heartache are not the last word. At the end of his Chronicles of Narnia, C. S. Lewis depicts heaven as the ultimate liberation from the relativity of experience. Here creatures cannot feel deprived, depressed or anxious. There is no adaptation-level trauma, for happiness is continually expanding. Here is "the Great Story, which no one on earth has read: which goes on for ever: in which every chapter is better than the one before." This resurrection hope does not eliminate the ups and downs of day-to-day life, but it does offer a liberating cosmic perspective from which to view them. To paraphrase Ruben Alves, the melody of the promised future enables us to dance even now. As a folk hymn of the St. Louis Jesuits puts it:

Though the mountains may fall,
    And the hills turn to dust,
Yet the love of the Lord will stand
    As a shelter to all who will call on his name;
Sing the praise
    And the glory of God.

Here on earth we will never completely escape the hedonic treadmill. But by pausing to recall the deprivations of our more distant past, by recognizing the relativity of happiness, by cutting our poortalk, by consciously selecting our comparison groups and by viewing life from the perspective of resurrection faith, we can begin to experience the radical liberation of the psalmist: "The LORD is my shepherd; I have everything I need" (Ps 23:1 TEV).

11
Liking
and
Loving

WHY DO WE LIKE SOME people more than others? Do birds of a feather flock together, or do opposites attract? Are old friends, like old shoes, the best, or does familiarity breed contempt? Such questions are central to our social lives, for our likes and dislikes play a vital role in whom we befriend and whom we marry, in where we choose to live and even in what church we join. Let's look at what social psychologists have learned about liking and loving and then see what this means for our interpersonal relationships.

Is Beauty Only Skin-Deep?
Does physical attractiveness significantly affect how much we like others? Most of us deny it. Oh, certainly, we would admit noticing how others look. But a major impact on how we feel about a person? Hardly. We manage to rise above the

superficial. Beauty is, after all, only skin-deep.

When college students are asked, for example, about the qualities which are important in their dating preferences, "looks" ranks near the bottom. Physical appearance is secondary to "personality," "character" or "sincerity." A host of social psychological studies reveal, nevertheless, that physical appearance *powerfully* affects how we evaluate other people.

One of the early studies looked at its role within dating relationships. Students at the University of Minnesota were randomly matched by computer for blind dates to a Welcome Week dance.[1] They had all been previously given a battery of personality and aptitude tests. On the night of the blind date, the couples danced and talked for more than two hours and then took a brief intermission to evaluate their dates. Which factors determined whether they liked each other? Was it intelligence, maturity or social skills? No, not at all. The one determinant of whether the guy liked the gal was her looks (which had been rated by the researchers beforehand). Likewise, gals liked handsome guys best.

While we might think that attractiveness influences only first impressions, psychologists have discovered that physical attractiveness is positively related to both frequency of dating and feelings of popularity. Even more intriguing is the fact that we tend to marry others who are about as good looking as we ourselves are. As James Dobson has pointed out, in the dating game men soon learn that "if at first you don't succeed, try someone a little bit homelier."

The importance of physical attractiveness is not limited to dating relationships. For example, college students judged an essay to be of higher quality when written by an attractive than an unattractive author. Similarly, simulated juries conferred less guilt and punishment on physically attractive defendants than on unattractive defendants. And in a recent study Ralph Keyes found that the average salary of over 17,000 middle-aged men was positively related to their height.[2] Since every inch over 5' 3'' was worth an extra $370 a year in salary, it appears that if you walk tall you'll carry a fatter wallet.

Most researchers are now convinced that a widespread physical attractiveness stereotype exists: attractive people are assumed to possess a variety of desirable qualities. When Karen Dion and her colleagues showed college students photographs of other college-age people, the more attractive were guessed to be happier, more intelligent, more sociable, more successful, more competent.[3]

The stereotype extends to adults' evaluations of children. In one study, for example, over four hundred fifth-grade teachers evaluated attractive children as having greater intelligence and scholastic potential than unattractive children. And as early as nursery school, children themselves are responsive to the physical attractiveness of their peers. It has been suggested that parents may implicitly teach the physical attractiveness stereotype through the bedtime stories they read their children. Physical deformities and chronic illness often symbolize inner defects. The villain in "Peter Pan," Captain Hook, wore a prosthesis. Cinderella's mean stepsisters were ugly. Hansel and Gretel were victims of an arthritic witch. Pinocchio's nose lengthened as his integrity slipped.

The stories are too good not to tell. But perhaps in reading them we should also use the occasion to teach our children that physical appearance is not the yardstick for measuring character or worth. Reflecting on contemporary fictional characters makes one wonder: May some of our children's more recent heroes such as E.T. and the Cookie Monster, who are scary yet lovable, serve to weaken the physical attractiveness stereotype? Certainly all of us need to become more conscious of how often we use children's physical appearance to evaluate them. "Mary, you look so nice! And isn't that a new dress? My, you *are* an angel!" or, "Billy, just look at yourself! Your hair's not combed, your plaid shirt and checkered pants don't match. What will people think?" How much better to say, "Tim, how helpful you are!" or "Barbara, you are a hard worker."

Does Familiarity Breed Contempt?

In 1972 the residents of a small coastal town in Ecuador were faced with the question of what to do with their new mayor, Pulvapies. Pulvapies had been elected fairly. In fact, he had defeated his closest opponent by a wide margin. There was one problem, however: Pulvapies was a foot deodorant! During the campaign the manufacturer had plastered billboards and distributed brochures with the words "FOR MAYOR: HONORABLE PULVAPIES." The manufacturer never dreamed the well-publicized foot deodorant would be elected.

The election illustrates a result of recent studies: quite contrary to the old proverb about familiarity breeding contempt, familiarity breeds fondness. Mere repeated exposure to all sorts of novel stimuli—nonsense syllables, Chinese characters, faces—boosts people's ratings of such stimuli. For example, Robert Zajonc found that when he presented the unfamiliar word *dilikli* to American subjects, they usually said it meant something unfavorable.[4] However, the more the word was presented, the more inclined subjects were to attribute a favorable meaning to it.

Familiarity through exposure also increases the attractiveness of people. Some years ago a mysterious student attended a speech class at Oregon State University enveloped in a big black bag. Only his bare feet showed. The instructor, who alone knew the bag's contents, reported that the attitudes of other class members slowly changed from hostility to curiosity and finally to friendship. Similarly, Canadian preschoolers who had watched two brief Sesame Street excerpts featuring North American Indians and Japanese-Canadians were more likely than children not exposed to express a desire to play with such children. Other things being equal, the more times people see a stranger, the more the stranger is liked.

This exposure effect may account for the intriguing finding that apartment dwellers are more likely to become friends with their next-door neighbors than with those just two doors away. It may also explain why instructors' classroom seating charts can determine friendship patterns rather dramatically. Interestingly enough, sociologists have long noted that geographic proximity reliably predicts our choice of marriage partners. There is some truth in the old adage that somewhere in this world there is one true love just for you— and the chances are that he or she lives only a few blocks away.

Do Birds of a Feather Flock Together?

Birds of a feather do flock together. In fact, few findings in social psychology have been confirmed with such regularity. Friends, engaged couples and spouses are very likely to share common attitudes, values and even personality styles. Among married couples, the greater the similarity between husband and wife, the more likely they are to be happily married and the less likely they are to divorce. William Griffitt and Russell Veitch confined thirteen unacquainted men in a fallout shelter for a ten-day period.[5] From knowledge of their prior attitudes the researchers were roughly able to predict the patterns of liking among the men during their time together.

The attracting power of shared attitudes, interests and values is also the power that drives a wedge between people who are dissimilar. Not only do we find those with dissimilar attitudes and values to be unlikable, we also tend to judge them as unintelligent, ignorant, immoral and even maladjusted. Indeed, the editorial columns in our newspapers frequently illustrate that proponents of one side of an issue often suspect the sanity of those taking a position different from their own.

Interpersonal similarity can influence our treatment of others in important ways in a variety of settings. In an experimental court case involving negligent homicide, a defendant whose attitudes were dissimilar to those of the jurors was assigned a full two years more in prison than a defendant with attitudes similar to jurors. Studies have also shown that we are more likely to believe a witness, we are more likely to judge a husband and wife as suitable adoptive parents, we are more likely to approve someone's bank-loan application, and we are more likely to hire an applicant for a job *if* these persons' opinions are similar to our own. Even our judgments of another's job performance are likely to be more positive when the other's values and beliefs are perceived to be similar to our own.

To Have a Friend, Be a Friend?
Most of us have at some time been told that another person likes us. Our immediate response? A warm feeling of reciprocal affection. The notion that we like those who like us is hardly new. The ancient philosopher Hecato suggested, "If you wish to be loved, love." Ralph Waldo Emerson gave similar advice: "The only way to have a friend is to be a friend."

Studies confirm that being liked does make the heart grow fonder. James Dittes and Harold Kelley led student participants in small discussion groups to believe that their fellow group members either liked or disliked them.[6] Those led to believe they were liked were more attracted to the groups than those who believed they were disliked. Ellen Berscheid and her colleagues even found that University of Minnesota students liked a fellow student who said eight positive things about them more than one who said seven things positive and one negative.[7] Apparently we are very sensitive to the slightest criticism received from others.

Evidence indicates that the greater our insecurity and self-doubt, the fonder we will grow of the person who likes us. Elaine Walster provided Stanford University women with either favorable or unfavorable analyses of their social sensitivity, thus offering an affirming boost to some while temporarily wounding the self-esteem of others.[8] Each was then asked to evaluate several people including an attractive male accomplice who just before the experiment had struck up a warm conversation and asked for a date. Which women most liked the man? Those whose self-esteem had been temporarily shattered and who were presumably hungry for social acceptance. Apparently approval after disapproval can be powerfully rewarding.

The Reward Principle

Many psychologists as well as philosophers and theologians believe we are naturally attracted to what rewards us. In other words, we like to be with and befriend people whose words, actions or mere presence brings us pleasure and satisfies our needs. We prefer to avoid those who make us feel uneasy, distressed, or who outright punish us.

So the aesthetic delight of physical beauty is likely to attract us to the lovely; those who are fat or pale, deformed or disfigured, however, repel us somewhat. Strangers are likely to elicit feelings of apprehension and uncertainty; those familiar to us bring comfort and security. Those who share our own opinions bolster our feelings of competence; those who disagree with us raise the unpleasant possibility that we ourselves are to some degree stupid or misinformed. Those who like us assure us of our value; those who don't challenge our worth. Lewis Smedes has observed that even our most important relationships contain the expectation that the other person will meet a need or provide some reward.[9] Romantic love may involve self-giving, but it always expects the other to provide a return on the investment. Similarly, friendship is born of the need for someone to be there with us, to support us, to trust and care for us. Even our love for God, says Smedes, is based on the fact that he promises to fill our soul's potential.

Does such "need-love," as C. S. Lewis describes it, have any legitimate place in the Christian's life? Isn't it merely poorly disguised selfishness? A reflection of immaturity at best?

One of Scripture's first lessons is that by ourselves we are incomplete. "It is not good that the man should be alone" (Gen 2:18 RSV). We need others to fill the emptiness within us. We are created social, not self-sufficient. "We are born helpless," observes C. S. Lewis. "As soon as we are fully conscious we discover loneliness. We need others physically, emotionally, intellectually; we need them to know anything, even ourselves."[10] The Bible does not denigrate need-love but, on the contrary, affirms it as natural and God-given.

Romantic attachments, brotherly affection and intimate friendships are the grist for the Old Testament's most memorable stories. Jacob labors a second seven years to win the hand of Rachel; Joseph holds Simeon ransom for a reunion with Benjamin; Jonathan risks his father's wrath and his own life in devotion to David. And what factors were important in the formation and maintenance of those close personal relationships? Physical beauty, similarity and mutual affection.

Rachel's physical beauty captures Jacob's attention: "Leah had weak eyes, but Rachel was lovely in form, and beautiful. Jacob was in love with Rachel" (Gen 29:17-18 NIV). Joseph and Benjamin shared the same mother: "[He] saw his brother Benjamin, his own mother's son. . . . Deeply moved at the sight of his brother, Joseph hurried out and looked for a place to weep" (Gen 43:29-30 NIV). And Jonathan sought reassurance of reciprocal love: " 'But show me unfailing kindness . . . so that I may not be killed. . . .' And Jonathan had David reaffirm his oath out of love for him" (1 Sam 20:14, 17 NIV).

The relationships that emerge from natural love in the Old Testament are often beautiful; they strengthen rather than debilitate, sustain rather than destroy. Love for Rebekah sup-

ports Isaac in the moment of his mother's death. More than
once Jonathan's friendship saves David's life. And through
her attachment to Naomi, Ruth becomes a part of redemptive
history.

Friendship was also a significant part of Christ's life. In
the intimacy he enjoys with Mary, Martha and Lazarus,
Christ further affirms the value of friendship and provides
evidence of his true humanity. The three at Bethany occupy
an important place in his life. Informed of Lazarus' death, he
says to his disciples, "Our friend Lazarus has fallen asleep;
but I am going there to wake him up" (Jn 11:11 NIV). And, arriving at the grave of his friend, Jesus is deeply moved; he
weeps. The Bethany townsfolk recognize the special relationship: "See how he loved him!" (v. 36).

In beginning his ministry, Jesus calls twelve men to be his
close companions. From this band he selected an even more
intimate circle to share his moment of earthly glory and to
support him in his hour of greatest suffering. Jesus' love for
all did not prevent him from having a unique relationship
with one from within that tiny circle. Time and again we are
reminded of a disciple whom, in a special sense, Jesus
"loved."

Beyond the Pleasure Principle

There's no question about it. Our personal needs and satisfactions often lead us into a rich friendship and communion
with others. Yet clearly Christ presents us with an even more
challenging and inspiring vision of love. When we understand love in the light of the cross, we understand that love
is to be shown to the unlovely, to the unworthy and to those
who have nothing to offer in return. Christ is the incarnation
of a love that is self-denying rather than self-seeking, that
strives to give rather than to get, that seeks to fulfill rather
than be fulfilled. The command to love as Christ loves is a
call to active concern for others without demand for reward.
This demands that we transcend our natural inclination to

love only those who are rewarding, that we love even those who are unattractive, unfamiliar, dissimilar and unfriendly. In order to transcend our natural ways and love as Christ loves, we need the empowering of the Spirit, whose fruit in our lives is love (Gal 5:22).

Our Lord rejected love based merely on reciprocated affections. "What credit is that to you? Even 'sinners' love those who love them, . . . do good to those who are good to [them], . . . and . . . lend to those from whom [they] expect repayment" (Lk 6:32-34 NIV). Being a follower of Jesus means much more. In fact, Jesus turns the principle of reciprocity upside down: "Love your enemies, do good to those who hate you, bless those who curse you, pray for those who mistreat you" (Lk 6:27-28 NIV). We are to turn the other cheek to those who assault us and lend to our enemies without expecting to get anything back. Jesus calls us to be sons and daughters of the Most High who "is kind to the ungrateful and wicked" (Lk 6:35 NIV). If there is anything that sets God's love apart from our natural inclinations, it is his capacity to love the unloving.

We have seen how we naturally migrate toward those who are familiar and similar. And that is not to be condemned. In chapter eight we argued that developing and maintaining a Christian lifestyle demand seeking out those who share similar values and thereby recapturing the fellowship of the early church described as a "circle of friends." This emphasis on communal support, however, is not a call to withdraw from the world. The church is not first of all a therapy group. Nor is it a social club. The community exists not simply to serve the people within, but to serve and to minister to those not yet a part. The call had already come to the Old Testament community: "Love the stranger." And in the New Testament believers are admonished, "Do good to all men" (Gal 6:10 RSV).

How difficult God's people have found that command! While the promise given Abraham was clearly intended to benefit *all* nations, this vision was lost by New Testament times.[11] Jesus reminds his hometown residents, members of the Nazareth synagogue, that there were many hungry Israelite widows in Elijah's time, but to whom was he sent? To a Gentile in Sidon. There were many lepers in Israel in Elisha's day. But whom did he cure? Naaman, a foreigner. How does the crowd react to Jesus' history lesson? They try to shove him over a cliff.

Time and again Jesus loves the stranger. Whom does he heal? A Syrophoenician woman's daughter, a Gerasene demoniac and the daughter of a Roman centurion. To whom does he first reveal himself as the Messiah? A despised Samaritan adulteress. With whom does he share supper? Zacchaeus, an outcast tax collector. The lesson that God's love extends to all could not have been more vivid, more dramatic. Yet even Peter needed a reminder. Coming to him in a vision, God teaches Peter that no one is unclean (Acts 10:9-16). God's love comes to foreigners as well as to the children of Abraham.

As Christians we are also called to transcend the pull of physical attractiveness. Our natural but inappropriate tendency to judge others on the basis of their appearance is highlighted in an interesting Old Testament account. Thoroughly exasperated with the disobedient Saul, God tells Samuel to anoint a new king over Israel. That new monarch is to come from the house of Jesse. Rightly fearing Saul, Samuel reluctantly follows God's instructions and goes to Bethlehem, saying he wants to offer a sacrifice. Although the old prophet is undoubtedly eager to complete his assignment as quickly and as unobtrusively as possible, God draws out the ceremony and uses the occasion to teach both Samuel and us a lesson in "seeing" (1 Sam 16:1-13).

Having called Jesse's family to the sacrifice, Samuel immediately sizes up the sons. Noting the splendid physical appearance (particularly the height of Eliab, Jesse's eldest son, Samuel anticipates God's pick. But, no, God tells Samuel,

"He's not the one." He continues, "I don't look at people the way you do: I see differently. You look at physical appearance but I look at the heart." So Jesse presents his seven oldest sons to Samuel, but God tells Samuel that he has chosen none of these. Finally, they fetch the least likely candidate, the youngest son, David, who was out keeping the sheep.

Loving others the way God does is not easy; by nature we are primarily motivated to satisfy our own needs. What then disposes us to pray for our enemies and forgive those who despise us? What disposes us to reach out to the ugly and disagreeable, to befriend the stranger, to approach and nurture those who evoke our natural repulsion? What prompts us at times to be more concerned about loving than being loved? What drives us to help others who can never return our love—or even know it was we who helped them? The power to practice such love is the power of God himself working in us. As Lewis Smedes notes, "If we have even a fleeting impulse to forget our own self-interest and act solely for another, with no regard for any reward, we are in touch with the core of cosmic reality."[12]

12
And Who *Is* My Neighbor?

ONE OF THE MOST memorable pictures Scripture gives of love that is self-denying rather than self-seeking is Jesus' parable of the good Samaritan. When Jesus was asked, "And who is my neighbor?" he told the story of how, after a priest and a Levite passed by a man who lay beaten and robbed on the road to Jericho, a despised Samaritan showed compassion (Lk 10:29-37). By offering his time and money, at great personal cost and contrary to social mores, the Samaritan exemplified the sort of altruism studied by social psychologists. In fact, the parable itself provided the direct impetus for an experiment.

Too Busy to Help?
Reflecting on the parable, psychologists John Darley and Daniel Batson speculated about the possible differences be-

tween the unhelpful priest and Levite and the helpful Samaritan.[1] Why didn't the first two stop and help? The priest and Levite were prominent public figures who were perhaps hurrying to their appointments while glancing furtively at their sundials. The lowly Samaritan was probably in much less of a hurry. He no doubt had far fewer and less important people counting on him to be at a particular place at a particular time. To see if "good" people in a hurry do indeed act as the priest and Levite did, Darley and Batson recreated the situation described in the parable.

After being asked to deliver a brief talk, which for half the participants was actually on the good Samaritan parable, Princeton Seminary students were directed to a recording studio in another building. While in transit, each passed a victim slumped in the alley, head down, eyes closed, coughing and groaning. Some of the students had been sent off knowing they had plenty of time: "It'll be a few minutes before they're ready for you. If you have to wait over there, it shouldn't be long." Of these, most stopped to offer aid. Others, however, had been told, "You're late. They were expecting you a few minutes ago so you'd better hurry." Of these only 10 per cent offered help. Conclusion? Hurried people are likely to pass by someone in distress, even if they are hurrying to speak on the parable of the good Samaritan.

The difference in helping between the two groups of seminarians is clearly not due to callousness. It can only be explained in terms of differences in time pressure. One group was in a hurry; the other was not. Of those seminarians in a rush, a few did not even see the victim. Most noticed, however, and went on by. But they did not consciously choose to ignore the victim's distress. Rather, because they were in a hurry, they simply passed by without thinking about it. Their minds were on the speech they were to make. A few seminarians were aroused and anxious after the encounter in the alley. They realized the man's plight but also felt committed to helping the experimenter. In genuine conflict they hurried on because of their devotion to duty.

Busyness can be an obstacle to helping others. The pressures of daily living—of getting to class or work on time, of making that next appointment, of preparing for that next test, of completing that paper—may prevent us from noticing or pausing to reflect on the needs of those around us and how we might help. While I was outlining this chapter one fall Saturday afternoon, my wife suggested that we visit a neighbor suffering from multiple sclerosis, now hospitalized. Ironically the words almost fell out: "Not today. I'm too busy writing 'Who Is My Neighbor?' "

We are people in a hurry. We have jobs to do. We intend to do them well and want to be uninterrupted. The homework must get done, the checkbook must be balanced, the floors waxed, the letters written, the lawn mowed. We perform our duties and "pass by on the other side."

Note that our problem is not necessarily selfishness. The seminarians in Darley and Batson's study were not rushing to play cards in the student union. They were on their way to retell the parable of the good Samaritan! Nor were the priest and Levite likely hurrying to Jerusalem for the premier showing of *Rocky IV* or the annual synagogue picnic. They were possibly headed for the Temple—perhaps to chair a meeting of the Subcommittee to Improve Jewish-Samaritan Relations? Or was it to kick off the Tenth Annual Drive to Repair the Jericho Road?

Even within the church we maintain a frenzied pace. We have committee and council meetings to attend, lessons to be taught, programs to be kept running, sermons to be preached. Sometimes the result is that we don't see others around us clearly, even our own parents, mate or children. Other times we don't fully recognize the choices we make with our time, effort and talent. Most often the obstacle to compassion is not callousness; rather, like Martha preparing dinner, we get preoccupied with the task at hand, fulfillment of obligation, devotion to duty. Indeed, Luke puts Jesus' les-

son to Martha on choosing the better part right after the lesson of the good Samaritan. Don't interrupt us—we want to be
seen as good committee persons, hard-working elders, dea-
cons and Sunday-school teachers, effective ministers. Our
calendars are filled, our watch alarms set.

A hallmark of Christ's ministry was his willingness to be
interrupted. When the crowd tells Bartimaeus to hush, Jesus
stops, hears the blind beggar's request and heals. When the
disciples protect Jesus from the onslaught of children, he
beckons them closer, embracing them. Jairus interrupts his
preaching to ask him to come heal his daughter, and Jesus
follows. Traveling from Judea to Galilee, he hears the Samari-
tans' request to stay and remains two full days.

Busyness may be one obstacle to altruism. But that certainly was not the only lesson Jesus intended to teach in
relating the story of the good Samaritan. Was he teaching
that love is a norm, a principle by which we all should live?
The lawyer who asks "Who is my neighbor?" already knows
that love is a duty. In fact, he has just recited the law "Love
God and your neighbor as yourself." The lawyer, the priest
and the Levite already knew and professed verbally the law
or norm of love. So do we.

The parable is clearly one of contrasting behaviors, not
ideologies. Jesus teaches that professing love is not enough;
it must find expression in action. The Samaritan's *action*
made him neighborly; Jesus says, "Go and *do* likewise." Unfortunately, our professed standards often have little impact
on our actions. Although religious individuals think and
say they are more responsive to the needs of others, measures
of their *behavior* typically fail to support the claim.[2] Why?
Perhaps we just need frequent reminders? Darley and Batson
wondered if those who thought about the altruistic norms of
the good Samaritan parable might be more likely to help than
those who were thinking about job opportunities for seminary students. So some were assigned to preach on the good
Samaritan and some were not. But those in the first group

helped only slightly more frequently than those in the second.[3]

Compassion and Helping

A careful reading of the parable reveals something else: the perceptions and feelings of the priest and the Levite contrast sharply with the Samaritan's. The first two do not see the victim as a neighbor, and thus they pass by on the other side. The Samaritan perceives him as neighbor, experiences compassion and helps. The Samaritan has *empathy*; the priest and Levite do not.

Seeing a person in distress is emotionally disturbing to most people. Such emotional turmoil was demonstrated some years ago in a series of studies by Ezra Stotland.[4] An accomplice of the investigator pretended to experience pain while taking part in an experiment. Observers' blood pressure, heart rate and perspiration were measured while they watched the victim. When he showed signs of pain, the observers tensed and perspired. Studies showed that even infants evidence such reactions to others' distress; for example, newborns cry in response to the sound of another infant's cry—no mere echo either, but a vigorous, intense, spontaneous cry. Some psychologists have concluded that the capacity for empathy may be inherent.

Research indicates that empathy, the ability to imagine oneself in the place of others, promotes positive social action. In one recent experiment college students were asked to imagine that a friend was terminally ill, and they were instructed either to think about the dying friend's feelings or to reflect on their own reaction to the illness.[5] Later, when asked to do an anonymous favor for someone, those who had focused on their friend's feelings were much more likely to do the favor than those whose thoughts had been focused on themselves.

Other studies have also indicated that seeing or hearing "with feeling" leads to helping. Female students heard an accomplice scream that a stack of chairs was falling on her.[6] The greater a student's change in heart rate, the more quickly she intervened. Moreover, the physiological arousal preceded and did not merely accompany helping.

The film series *Roots* and *Holocaust* probably triggered more empathy for Black and Jewish suffering than any documentaries on slavery or the concentration camps. Each film took viewers into the experience of specific people with whom they could identify, who had thoughts, motives and feelings like their own. Inside someone else's skin, our perceptions change. A hunger-awareness dinner or day of fasting may alter attitudes and actions more effectively than a month of sermons. Taking adolescents into a nursing home to eat lunch with the elderly may generate more compassion than five Sunday-school lessons on the fifth commandment.

Neal Plantinga distinguishes compassion from mere sentimentality: "It is a knowing pity, a penetrating pity, a pity that has real understanding, an insight into the situation of another." Moreover, it can be fostered through alert, focused seeing. You deliberately *identify* with others. You deliberately *expose* yourself, deliberately *inform* yourself about the lives of others. He writes, "You try, you struggle, you make yourself see life from another's point of view. What is it to be married as loosely and trivially as she is? What does it feel like to know others are more popular than you? What is it in another that makes him or her feel obliged to impress you? You need to get far enough in another to understand, to experience with, suffer with another."[7]

Christ himself provides the model. As the Immanuel, or "God with us," he entered our lives to share our sorrow and pain. Throughout the Gospels, Christ is pictured as one who identifies with those in specific need. "Filled with compassion," Jesus heals the leper. And when he sees the widow at Nain, he is "moved with compassion" and raises her son. When the blind men ask for their sight, Jesus "had compassion on them" and touched their eyes. The compassion he shows us and the model he provides ought to encourage us to feel the pain of another, and to be moved to relieve it.

Seeing Similarities, Not Differences

Empathy seems to be facilitated by our perceiving another human as like us. As we saw in the last chapter, similarity produces bonds; the perception of differences creates barriers. In the Stotland empathy studies, observers responded more empathetically if they were led to believe the victim was similar to themselves. The perception of similarity seemed to heighten the subjects' sensitivity to the reaction of the other person and to make it easier for them to imagine they were in his or her place.

Compassion is rooted in a sense of human solidarity, in an awareness that we are all made of the same basic stuff. But that perception does not come easily. In fact, we generally define ourselves in terms of our differences, not our similarities. We attach greater value to our distinctiveness than our sameness. In response to the question "Who am I?" people are likely to mention their birthplace if they are foreigners, their ethnic membership when part of a minority, their hair color if red, and their sex when outnumbered by the other sex within their family. The church I attend is proud of its reputation as "an alternative" church. The college where I teach emphasizes its "distinctiveness" in attempting to recruit new students. Who are we, after all, if we can't point to something special, something distinctive, something that sets us apart from everyone else?

The experience of empathy, Harvey Hornstein observes, is closely tied to the human readiness to form bonds of *we* and barriers of *they*.[8] The most insignificant difference can prove to be the basis for organizing the world into a "we" and a "they." For example, Henri Tajfel and his colleagues created two groups in the laboratory by informing individuals that they tended to either underestimate or overestimate the number of dots flashed on a screen.[9] In a later task, each subject was asked to decide how a sum of money should be divided between two of his fellow subjects. The only information provided the subject about the recipient of the money was whether he was an overestimator or an underestimator. This trivial difference proved important in how subjects distributed the money: they tended to discriminate in favor of those similar to themselves and against those who were dissimilar.

Even within the Christian community the danger of dividing people into "we" and "they" is always present. Milton Rokeach laments, "Throughout history man inspired by religious motives has indeed espoused noble and humanitarian ideals and often behaved accordingly. But he has also committed some of the most terrible crimes and wars in the holy name of religion—the massacre of St. Bartholomew's, the crusades, the inquisition, Pogroms, and the burning of witches and heretics."[10] In explaining this "fundamental paradox" of religion, Rokeach argues that the church is simultaneously confronted with the tasks of teaching mutual love and respect, and perpetuating and defending itself against outside attack. In defending itself, distinctions between *we* and *they* become inevitable.

Fortunately, the spirit of authentic Christianity is one that recognizes the lesson of Christ's parable of the good Samaritan. Brotherly love is preached for those who are not biological kin. The very first pages of Scripture teach that God breathed his own breath into humankind, thus giving us a part of himself, making us the bearer of his own spirit and image. God's imprint on us demands that we look beyond another's race, nationality or sex, beyond another's achievement or failure. This is what marks us all as brothers and sisters, and provides the basis for our responding to one another in love. John Calvin writes that we have no reason to refuse a stranger who needs our aid because "the Lord shows him to be one to whom he has deigned to give the beauty of his own image." Clearly, a common Father unites us into one family.

Concern for the Feelings of Those We Help

Empathy helps us translate God's command of love into action. But it is important for another reason as well. If we just adhere legalistically to the law of love without feeling any true compassion, we end up focused on ourselves rather than on others. Helping becomes a response to a rule or to our own need to love rather than to others' needs. One result is that the aid given may be inappropriate. Empathetic helping responds to another's situation, another's suffering. It recognizes the effects aid has on the recipient. Compassionate Christians not only help but are sensitive to the effect aid has on recipients.

We often become insensitive to others' wishes, for example, whether they want to be helped at all or how they feel they can best be helped. Even in our helping we can treat people as objects! In the good Samaritan study, Darley and Batson examined not only whether people stopped to help but also the nature of the help they offered. Of those who stopped to assist the victim, some seemed to ignore his repeated statement that he was really quite all right, that he just needed to rest a few moments, that he preferred to be left alone. Others seemed to be more responsive to the victim's wishes. Of special interest was the finding that those who professed to be most religiously devout were those least responsive to the victim's desires. A more recent study reproduced this finding, reporting that the religiously devout were as likely to offer help when it was not wanted as when it was.[11]

Being a recipient of help can be a mixed blessing. Accepting a gift can damage dignity. Aid brings with it psychological costs, and many impoverished people may avoid seeking help to preserve a sense of self-esteem. In the request for aid often lies the admission that one is dependent and that the donor is superior.

Aid that is given out of a need to be helpful may be aid that seeks to keep others dependent. Only if others continue to need my help can I see myself as a strong, capable, loving person. Perhaps this explains why within the church we sometimes seem to want to do things *for* people rather than *with* them. William T. Cunningham, founder of Focus:Hope, an interracial organization that seeks to address problems of racism and poverty, has been critical of the church's attempt to deal with such issues. His complaint is not about the failure of the church to help, but about *how* the church has sought to help. "There is a strange thing pervading church leadership," he says. "It's the attitude that if I make the man equal, I'll be less. So instead I'll take care of him."[12]

C. S. Lewis has also observed how our need to help may lead us to keep others dependent. "The ravenous need to be needed," he writes, "will gratify itself either by keeping its objects needy or by inventing for them imaginary needs."[13] The aim of our giving, argued Lewis, should be to put the recipient in a state where he no longer needs our gift.

Have you ever received an unexpected Christmas present and had nothing to give in return? Or received a far more expensive gift than you gave? It can be most embarrassing. Giving others help they can't reciprocate may even threaten relationships. It makes them feel awkward. It creates unpleasant feelings of obligation. Under some conditions people may prefer a loan to an outright gift. While we must love with Christ's love, not motivated by the expectation of a return on our investment, we must also be *willing* to accept something back if it helps the recipient preserve his or her dignity.

Donald Kraybill suggests another way to preserve self-esteem: "When someone gives to me and says, I don't want anything back—just pass it on to someone else when you can, it releases me from indebtedness to the giver and still protects my self-dignity since I can reciprocate in due time to someone else. Suggesting that they pass the kindness on to

someone else when they can allows them to share in the re-
deeming process."[14]

The parable of the good Samaritan is clearly a call to compassionate action. Obedience requires that we transcend our
self-centeredness, even our busyness as we perform daily
(and good) tasks. Compassion is to be practiced unconditionally. Anyone in need is my neighbor and my brother.
Jesus makes it clear: We will be judged by how we have
responded to the sick, hungry, thirsty, naked, the stranger
and the prisoner. "I tell you the truth, whatever you did for
one of the least of these brothers of mine, you did for me"
(Mt 25:40 NIV).

13
Do Bad Things Really Happen to Good People?

COMPASSION IS NOT always our first response to suffering people, even to victims of gross injustice. When the British marched a group of German civilians around the Belsen concentration camp at the close of World War 2, one German is reported to have observed, "What terrible criminals these prisoners must have been to receive such treatment." Many of us have a similar tendency to believe that the world is a just place in which people not only get what they deserve but deserve what they get.

Social psychologist Melvin Lerner has found that most of us need to believe that "I am a just person living in a just world."[1] From early childhood, argues Lerner, we are taught that good is rewarded and evil is punished. Success comes to those who do what's right, and suffering to those who don't. Hard work will pay off; laziness will not. Belief in a just world is, of course, an important force for social stability. The consequences of children and adults' believing in a world where wicked people are rewarded and innocent people punished would be disastrous.

According to Lerner, people do care about justice for others as well as for themselves. This concern may, under certain circumstances, motivate people to help each other and to seek to remedy or to eliminate what they perceive as injustice. However, the desire for a just world may also, rather ironically, serve to perpetuate injustice. We may come to think that those who are rewarded must be good and that those who are punished must be wicked.

Blaming the Victim

One implication of believing "I am a just person in a just world" is that those who inflict suffering on others will begin to value their victims less. People not only hurt those they hate, but they come to hate those they hurt. In effect, the aggressor justifies his or her action by derogating the injured party. We can continue to see ourselves as just if our victims deserved what happened to them, either because they brought it on themselves or because they are despicable persons. Thus Hitler viewed Jews as "unfit" and portrayed them as the cause of Germany's problems. American military men viewed Vietnamese as less than human and considered killing a civilian equivalent to killing a water buffalo.

Innocent bystanders observing injustice also tend to conclude that victims deserve their fate. The reaction of the German citizen to the Nazi concentration camp confirms this. If in the minds of the German people those seized and executed by the Nazis were innocent, then it would follow that the German government was cruelly unjust. To maintain their sense of justice, some Germans apparently convinced themselves that those sent to the concentration camps really deserved the treatment they received. Closer to home, the killing of four students from Kent State University by members of the Ohio National Guard in 1970 was quickly followed by the rumor that the bodies of all four students were covered with lice and that they were suffering from syphilis so far advanced they would have been dead in two weeks anyway.

Psychological studies have also demonstrated that the need to believe in a just world can lead observers to disparage innocent victims. The results of these studies throw light on why we permit social injustice to continue. Imagine you are participating along with some other subjects in a study on the perception of emotional cues.[2] By what appears random choice, one of the participants, an accomplice of the experimenter, is selected to perform a memory task. She is to receive painful shocks for any error made, while you and the other participants observe and note her emotional response. After watching her receive a number of painful shocks and react with what seems to be great pain, you are asked to evaluate her along several dimensions. How do you think you will respond? With compassion and sympathy? This is what one might legitimately expect. The results indicated, however, that when observers were powerless to alter the victim's fate, they tended to reject and devalue her.

Studies using a variety of situations have demonstrated that observers find a correspondence between what happens to people and what they deserve. When portrayed in the experimental setting, even victims of murder, accident and natural disaster are viewed as in some way responsible for their fate. And, interestingly, the converse is also true. Success is taken as an indication of virtue. In one study an employee was given a large bonus as the result of a *random* drawing. When informed of this, his coworkers nonetheless concluded that he had worked especially hard.[3]

Individual Differences
Some people, of course, believe "I am a just person living in a just world" more than others. A relatively simple paper-and-pencil test has been used to assess this.[4] Tests also show

that those who believe it more strongly are more likely to see victims as meriting their misfortune or "asking for trouble."

Prior to the 1971 national draft lottery, groups of nineteen-year-olds completed the Just World Scale. After listening to the radio broadcast of the lottery results, they rated their fellow group members along several dimensions. Many of them expressed greater sympathy and liking for those picked by the lottery than for those passed over. As the investigators point out, this "vote of sympathy" is not too surprising since the subjects themselves were in the lottery and in many cases also victimized. The reaction of subjects scoring highest on the Just World Scale, however, ran counter to this pattern. That is, they resented the men selected more than the unselected, regardless of their own fate in the lottery.

Does God Let Bad Things Happen to Good People?

This research is also relevant for Christians. Zick Rubin and Letitia Peplau found that both church attendance and belief in a personal God were strongly correlated with just-world thinking.[5] The inconsistency between our professed concern for social justice and our actual conduct may be due to our belief in a just world.

But consider how the Bible actually presents a modified view of such thinking. In a test of Job's faith God permits Satan to inflict terrible suffering on him. He loses his possessions, his children and finally his health. Job's friends, including Eliphaz, Bildad and Zophar, come to comfort him. How do they react to his suffering? All three perceive the world as a just place where people get what they deserve and, conversely, deserve what they get. "Cheer up, Job, nobody ever gets anything he doesn't have coming to him." Why? Because God blesses the righteous and punishes the wicked. Eliphaz asks Job, "Have you ever known a truly good and innocent person who was punished?" (Job 4:7 LB). In a similar way Bildad says, "God will not cast away a good man, nor prosper evildoers" (Job 8:20 LB). Job's friends can only conclude that his suffering is a result of his sin and try to persuade him to repent.

In the New Testament Jesus' disciples reflect the same attitude toward the man blind from birth. They inquire, "Rabbi, who sinned, this man or his parents, that he was born blind?" (Jn 9:2 NIV). In his response Jesus clearly disallows such just-world thinking. In the first verses of Luke 13, he again rejects the notion that the suffering of the Galileans or the death of those in the collapse of the tower in Siloam was due to their personal sin.

One reason why Christians may seem indifferent to social injustice is that they see no injustice. As Scripture itself illustrates, belief in a just world can proceed from, and be supported by, belief in a just God. Consequently Christians may in a variety of ways attempt to justify injustice rather than to correct it. Like Job's friends and Jesus' disciples, we may still view suffering as God's punishment for personal sin. Or we conclude from the story of Job that for Christians suffering is a test of their faith, intended to draw them closer to God; for unbelievers, it is God's attempt to transform them. A third variation is that God will balance present suffering with future reward—if not in this life, then in the next.

In any case, we err when we pretend to know God's will and fail to follow the command to "do justice, and to love kindness, and to walk humbly with [our] God" (Mic 6:8 RSV).

Our view of God and how he works in this world has important implications for our social attitudes. Believing in a just and active God seems to provide no assurance that we will act justly. Paradoxically, that very belief may contribute not to justice but to justification of the present. Christians need to recognize that God acts through his people. That is, God works his love and justice in this world through Christians' obedience to his Word. If we believe that God works in this world through us, we will be motivated to work toward greater social justice. Such activity is the proper result of belief in a just God.

Melvin Lerner thinks the belief in a just world may originate and develop at an early age. He maintains that through maturation and experience young children develop a "personal contract" with themselves. They "agree" to forgo immediate rewards and endure self-deprivation in exchange for greater rewards to be achieved through personal effort in the future. In forming this personal contract, they orient themselves to the world on the basis of what can be earned or *deserved* rather than on the basis of what can be obtained at the moment.

Lerner argues that since children need to believe that they will receive the outcomes they deserve, they are motivated to believe that others must also get what they deserve. Becoming aware that others do not get what they deserve would constitute a threat to the personal contract. So as long as people maintain the contract, they will care about whether they live in a just world. The concern for justice, says Lerner, has its basis, first of all, in a commitment to deserving one's own outcomes. Lerner states, "Personal deserving then is both conceptually and motivationally prior to justice for others." It follows that concern for the plight of others will often be overshadowed by concern for one's own outcomes.

There is a striking parallel between Lerner's notion and how some Christians view their relationship to God. Some Christians seem to regard faith as a negotiating tool or bargaining chip with God. They agree to hold certain beliefs and even to conduct themselves in certain ways in exchange for God's favor. Fundamental to this kind of faith is the belief that "God will bless me if I am good and punish me if I am bad."

The attempt to merit God's favor becomes most obvious, of course, when we are in greatest need. Not only do our prayers become more fervent, but we become conscious of conforming our lifestyle to God's will. Miron Zuckerman recently reported a series of ingenious experiments in which he demonstrated that, in time of personal need, those with a strong belief in a just world were significantly more responsive to requests for help.[6] They would give aid even if the assisted people could in no way reciprocate. Zuckerman reasoned that, by responding to the need of another, helpers hoped to earn or deserve a favorable outcome themselves.

Typically, "faith as contract," like Lerner's personal contract, is future-oriented. I postpone immediate gratification in exchange for future reward. Living the Christian life is a "vale of tears" which will eventually pay off in God granting me salvation and eternal life. Implicit in such a reward-and-punishment theology is a commitment to personal deserving. Christians holding such a perspective fail to recognize that faith itself is a *gift* of God, and that in the work of Jesus Christ they have life *now*, abundantly. Mature Christians know that God's grace is unearned, and that the abundance comes in knowing him—not in what he gives.

Our relationship with God will likely become the model for our relationship with others. To the degree we view our relationship with God as a contract based on personal deserving, we are likely to be oriented toward personal deserving in our relationships with others. There will always be these questions: What consequences will my helping others have for me? Has the other person really earned my respect and my help? Is the need legitimate? To what extent is the sufferer responsible for his or her own misery?

Such a Christian misses the God of Scripture who commands that we protect the poor, the widow, the orphan, without asking how they became poor, widowed or orphaned in the first place. In short, this Christian's relationships with others will be no different from those of unbelievers who are first of all concerned about preserving a personal contract and living in a world where outcomes are deserved.

We are released from the chains of our just-world assumptions when we begin to realize that we honestly don't want what we really deserve. When we face our deep need and our just-as-deep unworthiness of getting that need met, we are ready for God's mercy. We are freed to gratefully receive what we haven't earned, the love of a just God who out of his abundance gave his Son to redeem us. Those who have experienced God's mercy and grace look on their social context with new eyes. Having been forgiven, they forgive. Having experienced grace, they are gracious in their dealings with people. Faith for them is not something they use to barter with God; it is a gift which shapes their lifestyle and attitudes toward others.

In simple obedience to God's Word and in gratitude for what he has done, we will love others without concern for the "rewards and costs" of such action, without asking whether others deserve our help and without wondering whether their needs are legitimate. The way God has loved us will provide the model for how we are to love others.

Justice: A Community Project

Lerner has demonstrated that the concern for a just world is a double-edged sword. I have emphasized here the less obvious, that is, how this desire for justice can perpetuate injustice. The need for a just world can also foster constructive social change, of course. Many attempt to reduce injustice.

Research indicates that the path which people ultimately follow—whether they seek to justify or to correct injustice—depends to a large extent on how available to them are the resources for eliminating the injustice. If people feel powerless or do not know what remedial action to pursue, they are more likely to justify the suffering of others. If, on the other hand, they can help and know how to provide assistance, they are more likely to seek to eliminate injustice. To persuade others that injustice exists without at the same time suggesting or providing the means to eliminate the injustice may be more detrimental than beneficial.

In recent years the church seems to have become more sensitive to, and concerned about, relationships between people as well as the individual's relationship to God. In many respects it is returning to the kinds of social concerns always evident in the historic church until this century. Concern for social justice is growing. But when the church preaches against injustice, it must at the same time develop specific programs to correct injustice. Otherwise, the response might be, "So what can I do about poverty, hunger, racial discrimination? Anyone in this land can make it if he really wants to. And if the leaders of underdeveloped countries were not so corrupt, they would have enough food to feed everyone." The person in the pew who is not provided guidelines on what can be done may end up justifying rather than trying to eliminate the injustice.

Finally, reducing injustice must be a community task. As we observed in chapter eight, we not only need each other to identify sources of injustice but also to develop and to support the means for alleviating it. Confronted with the magnitude of the problem, individuals quickly withdraw or, as we have seen, even deny its existence. We do not readily enter the world of victims alone. Research suggests that if we believe our resources will have only limited impact, then chances are we will avoid trying to help entirely.[7] Only by working together as a body of believers, sensitive to God's directive, can we mount an effective attack on injustice.

14
Blessed
Are the
Peacemakers

"BLESSED ARE THE peacemakers." A noble and agreeable thought. If anything should characterize our relations with others, it is peace.

But what is peace, and how can we make it? Here the agreement ends. Both Soviet and American leaders claim they seek peace. Both military spending proponents and disarmament advocates act in the name of peace. Guerrilla warriors are "freedom fighters" seeking a just peace; the military governments they oppose are trying to "maintain peace." Again, what is peace, and how can we make it?

The biblical vision of peace is two-dimensional. First, it is nonviolent, loving relationships. Jesus foresaw that we would suffer disagreements, sometimes to the point of seeing our neighbor as an enemy. Yet he counseled us to extend love even to those enemies. Shalom, the Old Testament word for peace, includes in its meaning physical, material, emotional and spiritual well-being. So the second dimension of peacemaking is to create the conditions necessary for Shalom, well-being.

People tend to focus on one dimension or the other—to become either peacekeepers (keeping things calm and "peaceful") or peacemakers (creating the conditions for well-being among those who do not have Shalom). Typically, the haves, who already enjoy well-being, are content with the economic and political institutions that provide their well-being and protect their peace. The have-nots more often feel a need for reform, for creating the conditions for improved well-being.

But why do the haves so often choose to keep rather than make peace? And why do both haves and have-nots find it so hard to love their enemies? As we look at these complex questions, we will see the interplay of several behavioral principles discussed already.

Justifying Injustice
Pope Paul VI has said, "If you want peace, work for justice." And what is justice? Most people think of justice as equity. When I perceive that the ratio of my outcomes to my inputs is equal to yours, I will consider the situation just; we both get what we merit. The key word here is perceive, however, for what I perceive to be equitable you may not. For example, in experiments those who are overrewarded—the haves—are much slower to notice the inequity than the underrewarded —the have-nots.[1] This sets the stage for conflict.

If compassionate haves do notice someone's misery, they may still be unmoved. Why? Why are good people so often tolerant of injustice? Part of the answer arises from the ironic just-world phenomenon. Believing that the world is just— that people deserve what they get—blinds us to injustice. If we infer from the high unemployment rate of young Black men that they must merit such a fate, then voilà! Justice reigns. Adversity is recognized; but if we can agree with Job's friends that the world is just and the adversity deserved, then we need not get upset about it.

Indeed, we might even blame the victims: "I made it without handouts, and they could too if only they had some ambition." To take an extreme case, slavemasters may likely view their slaves as having just those traits—laziness, irresponsibility—which justify continuing their slavery. So prejudice comes to reinforce the social and economic superiority of people with wealth and power.

This tendency is accentuated by another phenomenon, the *fundamental attribution* error. When we're observing other people's actions, our attention is on *them*, not on their situation; so we tend to attribute their behavior to their dispositions. When *we* act, however, our attention is more likely focused on the situation we are responding to. Thus we may infer that "Sharon is outgoing and Judy is shy. But with me it all depends on the situation." David Napolitan and George Goethals demonstrated this fundamental attribution error by having Williams College students talk with a young woman who acted either warm or aloof.[2] Half were told the truth—that for purposes of the experiment she was feigning either friendly or unfriendly behavior. Did the students use this information? No. If she acted friendly, they assumed she really had a friendly disposition. If she acted unfriendly, they assumed she really was an unfriendly person.

Similarly, haves may attribute unemployment or unfriendly behavior to people's "lazy" or "hostile" dispositions, while the people themselves blame it on social stress and injustice. Experiments suggest that if our perspective were to change, if we were to see the world through their eyes, our analyses would likely change as well.[3]

Being aware of these powerful tendencies is a necessary first step toward creating Shalom. If we realize that our perspective as outside observers focuses attention on the blameworthy characteristics of those who lack well-being, then we can purposely expand our perspective. Involving people from other economic classes within our fellowship circles, for example, will surely increase our empathy and help us to rejoice with those who rejoice and to weep with those who weep.

So that is one barrier to Shalom: The haves tend to justify and thereby perpetuate injustice. The task of biblical peace-making is to dismantle this barrier, enabling people to recognize injustice. The other task is to promote nonviolent, loving relationships by enabling people to see even their enemies as neighbors. Often we do the reverse, perceiving our global neighbors as our enemies.

The Stereotyped Enemy
We considered earlier several sources of distorted enemy images. The *self-serving bias* can seed prejudice in any of its several forms—racism, sexism, nationalism and other such deadly chauvinisms. "My group"—my race, my sex, my country—is presumed superior to yours. The tendency to *self-justify* further inclines people to deny the wrong of their evil acts. What is more, we filter and interpret information to fit our *preconceptions*.

Given these insidious phenomena, it is not surprising that people in conflict frequently form distorted, diabolical images of one another. To a curious degree, these distorted images are similar; they are mirror images. Each views the other as untrustworthy and evil-intentioned.

The war of words between the United States and the Soviet Union offers many examples of each side's attributing the same virtues to itself and the same vices to the enemy. Former Soviet Premier Brezhnev said that "American 'adventurism, rudeness, and undisguised egoism' threatened to 'push the world into the flames of a nuclear war.' " In a similar vein, the Soviet Defense Minister said that "the aggressive forces of imperialism, primarily the U.S.A., have led the intensity of their military preparations to an unusual level, are fanning the flames of armed conflict in different regions of the world, and irresponsibly are threatening to use nuclear weapons." Of their own motives, Brezhnev said, "I should like to emphasize that the essence of our policy is peaceableness, the sincere striving for equitable and fruitful cooperation." The words could as well have been spoken by President Reagan, who has often expressed mirror-image views; for example, "You often hear that the United States and the Soviet Union are in an arms race. The truth is, that while the Soviet Union has raced, we have not."[4]

Mirror imaging is supported and encouraged by each nation's ethnocentrism, the overevaluation of one's own group in comparison with other groups, especially those we perceive as rivals. A study sponsored by UNESCO just after World War 2 illustrates this tendency.[5] One thousand people from nine countries were given a list of twelve adjectives and asked to choose those that applied to themselves, the Americans and the Russians. All the national groups in the study agreed on one point: their own nation was the most peace-loving.

Ethnocentrism leads us to judge events in our world with a double standard, or to exhibit what has been called the mote-beam phenomenon. We overestimate the evil characteristics of the enemy and underestimate our own. After showing American fifth and sixth graders photographs of Russian roads lined with trees, a psychologist asked the children why Russians have trees along their roads.[6] "So that people won't be able to see what's going on beyond the road," and, "It's to make work for the prisoners" were the two answers received. And why did some American roads have trees along the side? "Oh," the children said, "For shade," or, "To keep the dust down."

Stereotyping also shapes our image of the enemy. A stereotype simplifies our world by providing a shorthand category for strangers. Its unfortunate effect is the tendency to overgeneralize and produce false images. We may assume that all

Soviet people are Communists when, in fact, only a fraction are. Or we may stereotype Russians as atheists, though in reality some ninety million people—more than five times the number of Soviet Communist Party members—belong to Christian churches.

Stereotypes contribute to ill feelings toward our neighbors because they substitute generalized images for accurate ones and thus serve to justify hostile behavior. If we consider the U.S.S.R. a nation of atheistic Communists, it becomes easier to distrust them, dislike them and assume they have evil motives. While we might consider it morally unthinkable to point nuclear warheads at a nation of people who eat, play and work like us, threatening the lives of our stereotyped enemy is another matter.

The dangers of forming an enemy image become clear when we examine how psychological factors fuel the arms race. Why do they propose arms control? For propaganda purposes. Why do we propose arms control? Because we desire peace. Our images may be true and theirs false. But, given the universal self-serving bias confirmed through research, it is more likely that our ethnocentrism and use of double standards lead us to disparage the enemy. Each nation states, moreover, that "our strategic nuclear weapons are defensive, whereas theirs are aggressive." And each nation selectively reports armaments to make its enemy appear the stronger. In the early 1980s we heard American leaders complain that "the Soviets have more land-based missiles and more nuclear megatonage." Russian leaders complained that "the Americans have more submarine and air-launched missiles and greater warhead accuracy." Thus both sides could justify their "needs" to build new, more devastating weapons. Small wonder that arms-control talks progress slowly!

The enemy image also promotes a willingness to use violence, even nuclear weapons. After we have characterized a group of people as "the enemy," it is natural and easy to dehumanize them. This tendency to transform the enemy into something subhuman allows a soldier to kill a fellow human being. People become Communists and fascists, Japs and gooks. Killing an ideology, especially one that appears to threaten our basic freedoms, is much easier than killing a familiar person.

The enemy image also supports the policy of deterrence. Deterrence seeks to prevent war with the threat that any attack will be met by an intolerable retaliation. Deterrence policies grow out of mutual distrust: you may attack me, since I know the kind of enemy you are, so I will build up my potential for counterattack. When both sides have this mirror image of each other and tend to misperceive the other's motives (you're aggressive; I'm defensive), there exist all the ingredients for an upward spiral of hostilities. Both sides say, "It looks like my enemy is in an arms race, preparing to gain the superior power necessary to attack me." Thus each defines its own behavior as increased "defense" spending in response to the other's attempt to gain nuclear superiority.

The following rhetoric, for example, reported by the Associated Press, could have originated with either the United States or the U.S.S.R. Who do you think was responsible?

(Reagan/Andropov) acknowledged (Washington's/the Kremlin's) military might had grown in the last decade, but said the (United States/Soviet Union) had been compelled to strengthen itself because of the "feverish (U.S.S.R./U.S.) effort to establish bases near (American/ Soviet territory)" and to counter "the (U.S.S.R./U.S.) military superiority for which (Moscow/Washington) is now pining so much."

In fact, Soviet leader Andropov is responsible for these words. But the words have a familiar sound when put in Reagan's mouth. As a result of such mirror images, hostilities increase rather than decrease. Moreover, the psychological dynamics involved in the strategy of deterrence—fear, distrust, misperception, threats—actually accelerate arming for

war. It is safer to risk the costs and dangers of an arms race
than to chance the enemy's cheating and gaining an attack
advantage. So the arms race spirals while, ironically, both
sides claim that peace and disarmament are their high priorities.

The Call to Peacemaking

We are called to be peacemakers. With so many barriers to
peace, however, the task may seem hopeless. Surmounting
so many obstacles would require a miracle! But talk about
miracles is more than a figure of speech for Christian peacemakers. The language of faith speaks of peace with miracle
language: peace is a gift from God; peace is part of the "new
creation"; peace comes from transformation, conversion,
discovery.

A familiar story told of St. Francis of Assisi illustrates the
miracle of peacemaking, especially in terms of the transformation of individual attitude change. St. Francis had always
felt a particular disgust for lepers. In fact, he panicked every
time he saw one! One day, walking along the road below
Assisi, he saw one of those disgusting lepers coming toward
him. His knees went limp, and as the leper came closer, the
odor of rotting flesh attacked Francis's sense so powerfully
that it seemed he was smelling with his eyes and ears as well
as his nose. But this time Francis did one of those surprising
things that only the power of Jesus' Spirit could explain.
Despite his revulsion, he reached out and touched the leper
—threw his arms around the leper's neck and kissed his
cheek—whereupon Francis's hatred was turned to love.[7]

St. Francis devoted much of his remaining life to bringing
Shalom, God's peace, into the empty lives of lepers. How can
we explain the change? His change in attitude was preceded
by a change in action: one day Francis kissed a leper. That act
established a new relationship in which Francis was able to
discover something new about enemies and, as a result,
about peacemaking.

Francis's experience fits in with the psychological principles we have been discussing. Perhaps Francis had concluded that lepers somehow deserved their fate, believing that "whatever is, is just." Maybe the leper was being punished for his sins, and any assistance would constitute interference with divine retribution. Perhaps Francis's image of this "enemy" was based on generalizations, stereotypes and folklore rather than on the real nature of lepers. Certainly Francis had dehumanized the leper, consigning him to a subclass of creatures. After all, one ran a risk of social rejection and contamination by establishing contact with a leper.

But Francis reached out to the leper and broke through the barriers that normally maintained the adversarial relationship. We can surmise that in doing so Francis recognized some of the key principles that are foundational for all Christian peacemaking.

First, contact with our enemies usually reveals a surprising discovery: they are real people with the same mixture of loves, hopes, concerns and sins that we have. An enemy may seem disgusting, but with a good dose of honesty we can recognize that we are not without our faults either. And as we recoil in self-defense ("Hey, I'm not all that bad when you get to know me"), we realize that the same truth applies to our enemies. This experience is a discovery of our *common humanity*. It turns upside down our common tendency to dehumanize enemies and reminds us that we are all God's creatures whom he loves and sustains. The distinctions, stereotypes and negative images we use to alienate ourselves from brothers and sisters in the human family are all less real than our unity with them. Paul explained that our divisions are erased in the unity of Christ: "There is neither Jew nor Greek [cultural and religious division], slave nor free [economic or class distinction], male nor female [sex difference], for you are all one in Christ Jesus" (Gal 3:28 NIV; see also Col 3:11).

Second, peacemakers aren't asked to deny the evil characteristics of others, but rather to respond with reconciling love. In the mystery of his transformation, Francis was moved to respond in a new way to the leper's disgusting characteristics. The new response was love and acceptance. This teaching of Jesus was so radically new that its novelty is still unsettling: But I say to you, love your enemies! (Mt 5:44).

Jesus replaced retaliation with reconciliation, introducing an entirely new way of relating to the neighbor who is "enemy." Jesus' own way of responding to those who opposed him provides the model, as Paul notes: "God shows his love for us in that while we were yet sinners Christ died for us. . . . While we were enemies we were reconciled to God by the death of his Son" (Rom 5:8, 10 RSV). The Christian makes peace as God does—through acts of reconciling love. We must do to our enemies not as they do to us, but as God has done to us in Jesus Christ.

Third, peacemaking involves risk. Kissing the leper was an act of courage, and Francis couldn't know what to expect. Nor can we. We cannot know what extending justice to the poor will mean for our own standard of living. We risk living with less. We cannot know in advance how our enemy will respond to our acts of good will, though when we remember that our enemies are more human and humane than our images of them, we need not be totally pessimistic. But Christian peacemakers must recognize in their endeavors the "risk of the cross." Among other things, the cross reminds us that good does not always meet with immediate success in a world where evil is a reality. But the empty cross is also a symbol of hope. Resurrection is an important part of peacemaking, serving as a reminder that on Easter morning God's verdict came down on the side of suffering love.

Part IV
Studying

PEOPLE ARE FASCINATING. We are all different. We are all alike. We are simple. We are complex. Learning more about people is something we all do throughout our lives, whether we are social psychologists or parents or farmers or stockbrokers. And the topic is never exhausted. There are always new discoveries to make. There is always something to learn about humanity.

In the past fourteen chapters we have looked at how one discipline, social psychology, approaches the study of human nature. Now we would like to turn the tables a bit and study social psychology. Should we study people in the way that it does? How legitimate is this method? What can be learned that we can't discover in other ways? What are its limitations? In answering these questions, we hope to put this book in the broader context of God's call for us to know him and his works.

15
Called
to
Understand

CHRISTIANS HAVE GOOD reasons to pursue scholarly inquiry into human nature and human relationships. As God's stewards in this world, we are called to understand and care for all of his creation, especially his people. The second table of the law makes knowledge and understanding of our interpersonal relationships paramount. Moreover, if our vocation is ultimately to know and serve God, and if John Calvin was right in saying that we can't have a clear knowledge of God without a corresponding knowledge of ourselves, then the pursuit of self-knowledge is indeed a religious duty. Probing the mystery of human nature is part of worshiping God with our minds. Christian psychologists thus see their study and research as a Christian activity.

Most books on psychology and religion have drawn upon

personality theory, psychotherapy and counseling. While
these are important areas, they actually represent only a
small part of psychology—perhaps two chapters out of twenty in an introductory text. Our goal here has been to intro-
duce a newer specialty, social psychology, and to consider
its implications for Christian faith and life. It is our hope that
these insights about human nature will be used to build up
the church in Christlikeness.

But Why a "Science" of Human Nature?

If the search for self-understanding is a Christian obligation,
then we should pursue the truth vigorously and on all fronts,
wherever it may be found. There is not a square inch of the
whole world of which God does not say, "This is mine," for
if God is anything he is the Creator—the author of all truth.
And believing that "all truth is God's truth," we need not be
afraid of what we find, no matter how surprising or unsettling the discovery may be. We have a final security from
which to survey everything with freedom and openness. Of
all people, we should be most attentive and open to new insights and to reformulations of our existing beliefs.[1]

Knowing that this is our Father's world motivates us to
search God's works as well as his Word. Scientific data are
part of God's truth as well as scriptural revelation, and thus
we respect the insights that come through both natural and
biblical revelation. This attitude has motivated scholars for
centuries. Contrary to the popular idea that science and religion are enemies, modern science was actually nurtured by
the Christian world view. Many of its founders—people like
Blaise Pascal, Francis Bacon and Isaac Newton—drew en-
couragement from the Bible. They believed that the creation
was God's good gift and that whatever they discovered was
ultimately his. Reflecting that same attitude today, we welcome the scientific study of human nature and social behavior. We see psychological research in Christian terms—as
one way of exploring God's general revelation.

The Ethics of Experimentation

None of this is to argue, of course, that the application of the scientific method to the study of human nature is without its pitfalls. Although our look at social psychology has not been comprehensive, the studies we have introduced are representative of how social psychologists do their work. They raise questions that do not usually occur in the scientific study of the nonhuman aspects of the world. Is it right to study people the same way we study behavior among zebras? Is it ethical to experiment with people to learn how we behave?

To obtain useful information about people's social behavior, researchers sometimes temporarily deceive and distress their participants. Perhaps the most controversial study described in this book is Stanley Milgram's investigations of obedience to authority in which he found the majority of average citizens willing to administer intense shock to another person in compliance with the experimenter's command. Not only were all participants temporarily deceived, but for many the experience was extremely stressful. Critics have argued that participants' self-concept may even have been altered. One participant's wife told him, "You can call yourself Eichmann."

In defending his study Milgram points not only to its important lessons and potential benefits for humanity, but also to the support he received from the participants themselves after the deception was revealed and the experiment explained. When surveyed later, 84 per cent said they were glad to have participated; only 1 per cent regretted volunteering. A year later, a psychiatrist interviewed forty of those who had suffered most and concluded that, despite the temporary stress, no one was hurt.[2]

Do the insights gained through research justify the discomfort caused participants? John Darley and Bibb Latané's famous studies of altruism also highlight the researcher's ethical dilemma.[3] To determine how the presence of bystanders may influence an individual's reaction to a call for help, Darley and Latané asked university students to discuss over a laboratory intercom their problems with campus life. To guarantee their anonymity, students were told they would not see each other nor would the experimenter eavesdrop. During the ensuing discussion, the participants heard one participant, the experimenter's accomplice, lapse into an epileptic seizure in which he pleaded for someone to help. Of those participants led to believe they were the only listener, 85 per cent sought help. Of those who believed four others also overheard the victim, only 31 per cent went for help. While these results are highly informative, participants had been deceived and most also found the laboratory experience stressful. Many of them had trembling hands and sweaty palms. Should the experiment have been conducted?

Two things should be said in defense of the researchers. First, they were careful to debrief their participants, explaining the experiment and its purposes. After this debriefing the experimenters also gave the participants a questionnaire. One hundred per cent said that the deception was justified and that they would be willing to participate in similar experiments in the future. None of the participants said they were angry at the experimenter. Other researchers similarly report that the overwhelming majority of subjects in such experiments say afterward that their participation was both instructive and ethically justified.

Some readers may ask if this is not a case of the-end-justifies-the-means thinking. The moral choice is not always clear, however, particularly when we must choose between the more positive of two goods or the lesser of two evils. When the choice is finally made, the critic can always counter, "Sounds like ends-justifying-means thinking!" (regardless of the choice made). Consider the example of Nazis inquiring about Jews in the attic. If the moral choice is to lie in order to preserve the lives of innocent people, can't the critic ask "So the end justifies the means?" The researcher has a twofold ethical obligation—to protect participants *and* to enhance human welfare. *Not doing* experimental research (even research involving temporary deception) also has ethical implications.

In recent years investigators have become increasingly sensitive to the well-being of those who volunteer for experiments. Ethical principles developed by the American Psychological Association presently require investigators to do the following:

☐ Tell potential participants enough about the experiment to enable them to give their informed consent.

☐ Be truthful and alert to alternative procedures to deception. If some other viable procedure can be found, it should be used.

☐ Protect people from harm and significant discomfort.

☐ Treat information about the individual participants confidentially.

☐ Fully explain the experiment afterward, including any deception. The only exception to this rule is when feedback would be brutal, making people think they have been stupid or cruel.

Psychologists, as indicated above, have a responsibility both to protect participants and to enhance human welfare by discovering influences on human behavior. Research guidelines must always recognize, as the above do, this twofold ethical obligation.

What Can We Learn from the Science of Human Nature?

We have attempted to show how social psychological research can inform and challenge individual Christians and the Christian community. As Arthur Holmes has observed, to believe that God's Word is the final rule of faith and conduct does not mean that *all* truth is either contained in the Bible or deducible from it.[4] Scripture is not an exhaustive revelation of everything to be known. Biblical revelation does not provide the content of politics, economics or engineering. And while it reveals the most important information about the human condition—our ultimate origin, our condition and our destiny—on scientific matters the Bible is obviously incomplete. Scripture provides no theory of human memory. It offers no analysis of persuasion, no conceptualization of group influence. While biblical revelation informs us that human judgment is clouded, it does not provide specific information on how people form and sustain false beliefs, nor on what contributes to effective group decision making.

Does this mean that biblical and scientific views of the person are totally unrelated, that one merely takes up where the other leaves off? Certainly not. Both make claims about human nature and offer propositions concerning observable experience. Both speak to the ways we think about, influence and relate to each other. Both are concerned with our self-perceptions, with conformity and independence, with loving and hating. If all truth is God's truth then all truth must be one, for God does not contradict himself. Since all revelation has its source in God, a fundamental unity exists between biblical and scientific accounts of human nature. They do indeed have common ground.

We have explored some of those significant connections. We have noted how the ancient biblical view of human nature as self-serving is receiving remarkable support from the emerging scientific view. In affirming and enlivening ancient biblical truths the "new" understandings of social psychology strengthen the credibility of biblical faith in this modern age. Seeing the parallels not only renews our appreciation for the biblical idea, but it prompts us to sharpen and clarify its meaning.

Those Points of Tension

But what about those possible points of tension? If all truth is one, why do inconsistencies sometimes exist between psychological and Christian understandings of human nature? And how do we resolve them?

In some cases conflict between scientific and religious accounts may be only apparent. Each account has its unique purpose, approach, focus and vocabulary. Operating at different levels, they may not be competing so much as complementary accounts of human nature.

We can view human nature and human relationships from a whole range of perspectives. Which viewpoint is most relevant will depend on the particular question we want answered. For example, in observing human aggression, a physiologist might note what changes in a person's brain state or blood chemistry typically accompany aggressive action.[5] A psychologist might note how frustration or the inability to achieve some specific goal in life often leads to aggression. A sociologist might study how social norms permit or restrict the expression of aggression within society. A theologian might describe aggression in terms of our alienation from God and one another.

Are these various perspectives in conflict? Not at all. Each provides a different way of looking at the same event. Each informs and contributes to our understanding of behavior, and one is not necessarily superior to the others. They complement rather than conflict with one another. Thus in identifying physical, psychological or social causes for human aggression, we need not deny that antisocial conduct has its basis in sin. Rather we more clearly understand sin's mechanisms. *All* the views are of interest to Christians.

In some cases, however, genuine conflict arises between psychological accounts and what we understand the Bible to be telling us. If psychology and Christianity are not to become insulated from each other, these points of tension will have to be explored and eventually resolved. We need, however, to understand the fallibility of both science and theology.

Contrary to its popular image, science is not as objective as most people think. Investigators don't merely read what's in the book of nature; their eyes are not mirrors humbly reflecting reality. We've already seen that one of the most significant facts about our minds is how much our preconceived notions bias the way we interpret the information that comes to us. Personal values shape the psychologist's choice of research topics, the questions raised, the methods applied and the interpretations given the data. Values are implicit in the very concepts of the discipline. A significant challenge therefore awaits Christian psychologists. They can be "salt of the earth" and "leaven in the loaf" by exposing concealed presumptions and hidden values. They can offer a perspective shaped by Christian beliefs and values.

However, just as scientific models of human nature are colored by the psychologist's presuppositions, so also is the theorizing of theologians subtly shaped by their underlying assumptions, background and personal values. This means we should be as wary to subject science to religious dogma as we are to conform religious beliefs to scientific inquiry. Either our psychological theorizing may be wrong or we may have wrongly interpreted Scripture. On occasion Christians have gained a more correct understanding of biblical truth by the revelations of scientific research. The insights of modern ecology, for example, have revolutionized our understanding of what it means to have dominion over the earth.

So both scriptural and scientific data are part of God's revelation to us, and we can respect the insights that come through either biblical or natural revelation. However, since our interpretations of both biblical and scientific data are colored by our presuppositions, we must be wary of absolutizing any human interpretation of Scripture or of nature. We view both through our own spectacles.

We hope this book helps bridge psychological research and Christian faith. The two are not enemies but allies. Having probed human behavior through recent research and seen its correspondence with Scripture, we want to encourage God's people toward effective Christian living: believing, influencing and relating with Christlikeness.

Notes

Chapter 2: Behavior and Belief

[1] Allan W. Wicker, "Attitudes vs. Actions: The Relationship of Verbal to Overt Behavior Responses to Attitude Objects," *Journal of Social Issues* 25 (1969): 41-78.

[2] See Amitai Etzioni, "Human Beings Are Not Very Easy to Change after All," *Saturday Review*, 3 June 1972, pp. 45-47.

[3] Jonathan L. Freedman and Scott C. Fraser, "Compliance without Pressure: The Foot-in-the-Door Technique," *Journal of Personality and Social Psychology* 4 (1966):195-202.

[4] Stanley Milgram, "Some Conditions of Obedience and Disobedience to Authority," *Human Relations* 18 (1965): 57-75. Although the victim was not actually shocked, this experiment has nevertheless been sufficiently controversial to serve as a stimulus for reforms in professional psychological research ethics.

[5] See Keith E. Davis and Edward E. Jones, "Changes in Interpersonal Perception as a Means of Reducing Cognitive Dissonance," *Journal of Abnormal and Social Psychology* 61 (1960):402-10; David C. Glass, "Changes in Liking as a Means of Reducing Cognitive Discrepancies between Self-Esteem and Aggression," *Journal of Personality* 32 (1964): 531-49.

[6] Jonathan Freedman, "Long-Term Behavioral Effects of Cognitive Dissonance," *Journal of Experimental Social Psychology* 1 (1965): 145-55.

[7] Ross D. Parke, "Rules, Roles, and Resistance to Deviation: Recent Advances in Punishment, Discipline, and Self-Control," in *Minnesota Symposia of Child Psychology*, ed. A. Pick, vol. 8 (Minneapolis: Univ. of Minnesota Press, 1974); E. Staub, R. Leavy, and J. Shortsleeves, "Teaching Other Children as a Means of Learning to Be Helpful," and E. Staub and W. Jancaterino, "Teaching Others, Participation in Prosocial Action and Prosocial Induction as Means of Children Learning to Be Helpful" (Manuscripts, Univ. of Massachusetts, Amherst, 1975).

[8] *Interpreter's Dictionary of the Bible* (Nashville: Abingdon Press, 1962), 3:44.

[9]Dietrich Bonhoeffer, *The Cost of Discipleship* (New York: Macmillan, 1963), pp. 69, 86.

[10]See W. A. Watts, "Relative Persistence of Opinion Change Induced by Active Compared to Passive Participation," *Journal of Personality and Social Psychology* 5 (1967): 4-15; and D. T. Ryan and R. Fazio, "On the Consistency between Attitudes and Behavior: Look to the Method of Attitude Formation," *Journal of Experimental Social Psychology* 13 (1977):28-45.

Chapter 3: The Inflated Self: A New Look at Pride

[1]E. Jerry Phares, *Locus of Control in Personality* (Morristown, N.J.: General Learning Press, 1976).

[2]Michael Ross and Fiore Sicoly, "Egocentric Biases in Availability and Attribution," *Journal of Personality and Social Psychology* 37 (1979): 322-36.

[3]Jean-Paul Codol, "On the So-Called 'Superior Conformity of the Self' Behavior: Twenty Experimental Investigations," *European Journal of Social Psychology* 5 (1976):457-501.

[4]See, for examples, Paul Slovic and Baruch Fischhoff, "On the Psychology of Experimental Surprises," *Journal of Experimental Psychology: Human Perception and Performance* 3 (1977):544-51; and Gordon Wood, "The Knew-It-All-Along Effect," *Journal of Experimental Psychology: Human Perception and Performance* 4 (1978):345-53.

[5]Margaret W. Matlin and David J. Stang, *The Pollyanna Principle: Selectivity in Language, Memory, and Thought* (Cambridge, Mass.: Schenkman, 1978).

[6]Neil D. Weinstein, "Unrealistic Optimism about Future Life Events," *Journal of Personality and Social Psychology* 39 (1980):806-20.

[7]Steven J. Sherman, "On the Self-Erasing Nature of Errors of Prediction," *Journal of Personality and Social Psychology* 39 (1980):211-21.

[8]See, for example, Lauren B. Alloy and Lyn Y. Abramson, "Judgment of Contingency in Depressed and Nondepressed Students: Sadder but Wiser?" *Journal of Experimental Psychology: General* 108 (1979):441-85.

[9]Peter M. Lewinsohn, Walter Mischel, William Chapline and Russell Barton, "Social Competence and Depression: The Role of Illusory Self-Perceptions," *Journal of Abnormal Psychology* 89 (1980):203-12.

[10]Barry R. Schlenker, "Egocentric Perceptions in Cooperative Groups: A Conceptualization and Research Review," Final Report, Office of Naval Research Grant NR#170-797, 1976.

[11]C. S. Lewis, *Mere Christianity* (New York: Macmillan, 1960), p. 25.

[12]Dennis Voskuil, *Mountains into Goldmines: Robert Schuller and the Gospel of Success* (Grand Rapids, Mich.: Eerdmans, 1983), pp. 147-48.

[13]Lewis, *Mere Christianity*, p. 99.

Chapter 4: Reasons for Unreason

[1]Barry Singer and Victor Benassi, "Fooling Some of the People All of the Time," *Skeptical Inquirer* 5 (2) (1980-81):17-24.

[2]Charles G. Lord, Lee Ross and Mark Lepper, "Biased Assimilation and Attitude Polarization: The Effects of Prior Theories on Subsequently Considered Evidence," *Journal of Personality and Social Psychology* 37 (1979):2098-109.

³Craig A. Anderson, Mark R. Lepper and Lee D. Ross, "Perseverance of Social Theories: The Role of Explanation in the Persistence of Discredited Information," *Journal of Personality and Social Psychology* 39 (1980):1037-49.

⁴Elizabeth F. Loftus and John C. Palmer, "Reconstruction of Automobile Destruction: An Example of the Interaction between Language and Memory," *Journal of Verbal Learning and Verbal Behavior* 13 (1973): 585-89.

⁵Daniel Kahneman and Amos Tversky, "Intuitive Prediction: Biases and Corrective Procedures," *Management Science* 12 (1979):313-27.

⁶P. C. Wason, "On the Failure to Eliminate Hypotheses in a Conceptual Task," *Quarterly Journal of Experimental Psychology* 12 (1960):129-40.

⁷B. F. Skinner, " 'Superstition' in the Pigeon," *Journal of Experimental Psychology* 38 (1948):168-72.

⁸William C. Ward and Herbert M. Jenkins, "The Display of Information and the Judgment of Contingency," *Canadian Journal of Psychology* 19 (1965):231-41.

⁹Ellen J. Langer, "The Illusion of Control," *Journal of Personality and Social Psychology* 32 (1975):311-28.

¹⁰Daniel Kahneman and Amos Tversky, "Judgment under Uncertainty: Heuristics and Biases," *Science* 185 (1974):1124-31.

¹¹Mark Snyder, Elizabeth D. Tanke and Ellen Berscheid, "Social Perception and Interpersonal Behavior: On the Self-Fulfilling Nature of Social Stereotypes," *Journal of Personality and Social Psychology* 35 (1977):656-66.

Chapter 5: Should We Believe in the Paranormal?

¹C. E. M. Hansel, *ESP and Parapsychology: A Critical Reevaluation* (Buffalo, N.Y.: Prometheus Books, 1980), p. 314.

²John Beloff, "Why Parapsychology Is Still on Trial," *Human Nature*, December 1978, pp. 68-74.

³H. A. Murray and D. R. Wheeler, "A Note on the Possible Clairvoyance of Dreams," *Journal of Psychology* 3 (1937):309-13.

⁴"Psychic Abscam," *Discover*, March 1983, pp. 10-11. See also James Randi, "The Project Alpha Experiment: Part I. The First Two Years," *Skeptical Inquirer*, Summer 1983, pp. 24-33.

⁵Singer and Benassi, "Fooling Some of the People."

⁶Fred Ayeroff and Robert P. Abelson, "ESP and ESB: Belief in Personal Success at Mental Telepathy," *Journal of Personality and Social Psychology* 34 (1976):240-47.

⁷See, for example, the following books which examine the reliability of Christian faith claims: Clark Pinnock, *Reason Enough*; Frank Morison, *Who Moved the Stone?*; F. F. Bruce, *The New Testament Documents: Are They Reliable?*; William Dyrness, *Christian Apologetics*; and Paul E. Little, *Know Why You Believe* (all published in Downers Grove, Ill., by InterVarsity Press).

⁸See, for example, Neal Oshterow, "Making Sense of the Nonsensical: An Analysis of Jonestown," in *Readings about the Social Animal*, ed. E. Aronson (San Francisco: W. H. Freeman, 1981), pp. 69-88.

Chapter 6: Is Anyone Getting the Message?

¹Thomas J. Crawford, "Sermons on Racial Tolerance and the Parish Neighborhood

Context," *Journal of Applied Social Psychology* 4 (1974):1-23.

[2]J. Martin, K. J. Patterson and R. L. Price, "The Effects of Level of Abstraction of a Script on Accuracy of Recall," paper presented at the Western Psychological Association Convention, 1979.

[3]William Strunk and E. B. White, *The Elements of Style* (New York: Macmillan, 1979), p. 21.

[4]John D. Bransford and Marcia K. Johnson, "Consideration of Some Problems of Comprehension," in *Visual Information Processing*, ed. W. Chase (New York: Academic Press, 1973), pp. 383-483.

[5]Lynn Hasher, David Goldstein and Thomas Toppino, "Frequency and the Conference of Referential Validity," *Journal of Verbal Learning and Verbal Behavior* 16 (1977):107-12.

[6]Norman Slamecka and Peter Graf, "The Generation Effect: Delineation of a Phenomenon," *Journal of Experimental Psychology: Human Learning and Memory* 4 (1978):592-604.

[7]Michael W. Traugott and John P. Katosh, "Response Validity in Surveys of Voting Behavior," *Public Opinion Quarterly* 43 (1979):359-77.

[8]William James, *Talks to Teachers on Psychology: And to Students on Some of Life's Ideals* (New York: Holt, 1922), p. 33. (Originally published 1899.)

Chapter 7: The Cost of Rewards
[1]Gordon W. Allport, "The Religious Context of Prejudice," *Journal for the Scientific Study of Religion* 5 (1966):447-57.

[2]B. F. Skinner, "Operant Reinforcement of Prayer," *Journal of Applied Behavior Analysis* 2 (1969):247, cited in Rodger K. Bufford, *The Human Reflex* (San Francisco: Harper and Row, 1981), p. 174.

[3]See, for example, Edward L. Deci and Richard M. Ryan, "The Empirical Exploration of Intrinsic Motivational Processes," in *Advances in Experimental Social Psychology*, vol. 13, ed. L. Berkowitz (New York: Academic Press, 1980), pp. 39-80.

[4]Mark R. Lepper and David Greene, "Turning Play into Work: Effects of Adult Surveillance and Extrinsic Rewards on Children's Intrinsic Motivation," *Journal of Personality and Social Psychology* 31 (1975):479-86.

[5]Patricia N. Middlebrook, *Social Psychology and Modern Life* (New York: Alfred A. Knopf, 1974), p. iv.

[6]Edward L. Deci, *Intrinsic Motivation* (New York: Plenum, 1975).

[7]Cline Seligman, Russell Fazio and Mark Zanna, "Effects of Salience of Extrinsic Rewards on Liking and Loving," *Journal of Personality and Social Psychology* 38 (1980):453-60. Sensitive to ethical concerns, the researchers debriefed all the participants afterward and later confirmed that the experiment had no long-term effects on the participants' relationships.

[8]Nicholas Wolterstorff, *Educating for Responsible Action* (Grand Rapids, Mich.: Eerdmans, 1980), p. 14.

[9]Edward L. Deci, *The Psychology of Self-Determination* (Lexington, Mass.: D. C. Heath, 1980), pp. 38-39.

[10]Michael Ross, "Salience of Reward and Intrinsic Motivation," *Journal of Personality and Social Psychology* 32 (1975):245-54.

[11]Edward L. Deci, John Nezlek and Louise Sheinman, "Characteristics of the Rewarder and Intrinsic Motivation of the Rewardee," *Journal of Personality and Social Psychology*, 40 (1981):1-10.

Chapter 8: Conformity: A Way Out

[1]Solomon E. Asch, "Studies of Independence and Conformity: A Minority of One against a Unanimous Majority," *Psychological Monographs* 70 (1956): whole no. 416.

[2]Quoted in *Psychology Today*, June 1974, p. 72.

[3]Stanley Milgram, "Some Conditions of Obedience and Disobedience to Authority."

[4]John Sabini and Maury Silver, *Moralities of Everyday Life* (New York: Oxford Univ. Press, 1982), pp. 35-53.

[5]Muzafer Sherif, *The Psychology of Social Norms* (New York: Octagon Books, 1965).

[6]Donald B. Kraybill, *The Upside-Down Kingdom* (Scottdale, Pa.: Herald Press, 1978), pp. 13, 16.

[7]Ibid., p. 302.

[8]Stanley Milgram, *Obedience to Authority* (New York: Harper and Row, 1974), p. 121.

[9]David G. Myers and George D. Bishop, "Discussion Effects on Racial Attitudes," *Science* 169 (1970):778-89.

[10]Andrew Kuyvenhoven, "Church Is People," *The Banner*, 2 February 81, p. 6.

[11]Arthur G. Gish, *Living in Christian Community* (Scottdale, Pa.: Herald Press, 1979), p. 141.

[12]Jim Wallis, "What Does It Mean to Be Saved?" *Sojourners*, May 1978, p. 12.

[13]Opinion expressed by Richard Foster in an address at the Yokefellow Conference, Richmond, Indiana, 1982.

Chapter 9: When Groupthink Strikes

[1]C. S. Lewis, *Screwtape Letters* (New York: Macmillan, 1959), p. 34.

[2]Irving L. Janis, *Victims of Groupthink*, 2d ed. (Boston: Houghton Mifflin, 1982).

[3]Ibid., p. 38.

[4]Ibid., p. 40.

[5]Ibid., p. 39.

[6]Ibid., p. 16.

[7]Richard L. Schanck, "A Study of a Community and Its Groups and Institutions Conceived of as Behaviors of Individuals," *Psychological Monographs* 43 (1932):2, whole no. 195.

[8]Howard A. Snyder, *Liberating the Church* (Downers Grove, Ill.: InterVarsity Press), p. 11.

Chapter 10: Why Do the Rich Feel So Poor?

[1]Philip Brickman and Donald T. Campbell, "Hedonic Relativism and Planning the Good Society," in *Adaptation-Level Theory*, ed. M. H. Appley (New York: Academic Press, 1971), p. 287.

[2]Philip Brickman, Dan Coates and Ronnie J. Janoff-Bulman, "Lottery Winners and

Accident Victims: Is Happiness Relative?" *Journal of Personality and Social Psychology* 36 (1978):917-27.

[3]Ibid.; see also Paul Cameron, *The Life Cycle: Perspectives and Commentary* (Oceanside, N.Y.: Dabor, 1977).

[4]B. G. Maslow, *Abraham H. Maslow: A Memorial Volume* (Monterey, Calif.: Brooks/Cole, 1972), p. 108.

[5]Marshall Dermer, Sidney J. Cohen, Elaine Jacobsen and Erling A. Anderson, "Evaluative Judgments of Aspects of Life as a Function of Vicarious Exposure to Hedonic Extremes," *Journal of Personality and Social Psychology* 37 (1979):247-60.

Chapter 11: Liking and Loving

[1]Elaine (Hatfield) Walster, Vera Aronson, Darcy Abrahams and Leon Rottman, "Importance of Physical Attractiveness in Dating Behavior," *Journal of Personality and Social Psychology* 5 (1966):508-16.

[2]Ralph Keyes, *The Height of Your Life* (Boston: Little, Brown, 1980).

[3]Karen Dion, Ellen Berscheid and Elaine (Hatfield) Walster, "What Is Beautiful Is Good," *Journal of Personality and Social Psychology* 24 (1972):285-90.

[4]Robert Zajonc, "The Attitudinal Effects of Mere Exposure," *Journal of Personality and Social Psychology Monograph Supplement* 9 (1968):1-27.

[5]William Griffitt and Russell Veitch, "Preacquaintance Attitude Similarity and Attraction Revisited: Ten Days in a Fall-Out Shelter," *Sociometry* 37 (1974):163-73.

[6]James Dittes and Harold Kelley, "Effects of Different Conditions of Acceptance upon Conformity to Group Norms," *Journal of Abnormal and Social Psychology* 53 (1956):100-107.

[7]Ellen Berscheid, G. William Walster and Elaine (Hatfield) Walster, "Effects of Accuracy and Positivity of Evaluation on Liking for the Evaluator," manuscript, 1969, summarized in Ellen Berscheid and Elaine (Hatfield) Walster, *Interpersonal Attraction* (Reading, Mass.: Addison-Wesley, 1978).

[8]Elaine (Hatfield) Walster, "The Effect of Self-Esteem on Romantic Liking," *Journal of Experimental Social Psychology* 1 (1965):184-97.

[9]Lewis Smedes, *Love within Limits* (Grand Rapids, Mich.: Eerdmans, 1978), pp. 128-29.

[10]C. S. Lewis, *The Four Loves* (New York: Harcourt Brace Jovanovich, 1960), p. 12.

[11]Kraybill, *The Upside-Down Kingdom*, pp. 230-57.

[12]Smedes, *Love within Limits*, p. 120.

Chapter 12: And Who Is My Neighbor?

[1]John M. Darley and C. Daniel Batson, " 'From Jerusalem to Jericho': A Study of Situational and Dispositional Variables in Helping Behavior," *Journal of Personality and Social Psychology* 27 (1973):100-108.

[2]For a review see C. Daniel Batson and W. Larry Ventis, *The Religious Experience* (New York: Oxford Univ. Press, 1982), pp. 252-99.

[3]Anthony G. Greenwald, "Does the Good Samaritan Parable Increase Helping? A Comment on Darley and Batson's No Effect Conclusion," *Journal of Personality and Social Psychology* 32 (1975):578-83.

[4]Ezra Stotland, "Explanatory Investigations of Empathy," in *Advances in Experi-*

mental *Social Psychology*, vol. 4, ed. L. Berkowitz (New York: Academic Press, 1969), pp. 217-314.

[5]William C. Thompson, Claudia L. Cowan and David L. Rosenhan, "Focus of Attention Mediates the Impact of Negative Affect on Altruism," *Journal of Personality and Social Psychology* 38 (1980):291-300.

[6]Samuel L. Gaertner and John F. Dovidio, "The Subtlety of White Racism, Arousal, and Helping Behavior," *Journal of Personality and Social Psychology* 35 (1977):691-707.

[7]Neal Plantinga, "Christian Compassion," manuscript, Calvin Theological Seminary, 1981.

[8]Harvey A. Hornstein, *Cruelty and Kindness* (Englewood Cliffs, N.J.: Prentice-Hall, 1976).

[9]H. Tajfel, C. Flament, M. G. Billig and R. P. Bundy, "Social Categorization and Intergroup Behavior," *European Journal of Social Psychology* 1 (1971):149-78.

[10]Milton Rokeach, "Paradox of Religious Belief," in *Personality and Religion*, ed. W. A. Sadler (New York: Harper and Row, 1970), p. 227.

[11]C. Daniel Batson and Rebecca A. Gray, "Religious Orientation and Helping Behavior: Responding to One's Own or to the Victim's Needs?" *Journal of Personality and Social Psychology* 40 (1981):511-20.

[12]Quoted in *Grand Rapids Press*, 30 January 1982, p. 1D.

[13]C. S. Lewis, *The Four Loves*, pp. 76-77.

[14]Kraybill, *The Upside-Down Kingdom*, pp. 213-14.

Chapter 13: Do Bad Things Really Happen to Good People?

[1]Melvin Lerner, *The Belief in a Just World* (New York: Plenum, 1980).

[2]Melvin Lerner and Carolyn Simmons, "The Observer's Reaction to the 'Innocent Victim': Compassion or Rejection?" *Journal of Personality and Social Psychology* 4 (1966):203-10.

[3]Melvin Lerner, "Evaluation of Performance as a Function of Performer's Reward and Attractiveness," *Journal of Personality and Social Psychology* 1 (1965):355-60.

[4]Zick Rubin and Letitia Anne Peplau, "Who Believes in a Just World?" *Journal of Social Issues* 31 (1975):65-89.

[5]Ibid.

[6]Miron Zuckerman, "Belief in a Just World and Altruistic Behavior," *Journal of Personality and Social Psychology* 31 (1975):972-76.

[7]Elaine (Hatfield) Walster, Ellen Berscheid and G. William Walster, "New Directions in Equity Research," in *Advances in Experimental Social Psychology*, vol. 9, ed. L. Berkowitz and E. (Hatfield) Walster (New York: Academic Press, 1976), pp. 1-42.

Chapter 14: Blessed Are the Peacemakers

[1]David M. Messick and Keith P. Sentis, "Fairness and Preference," *Journal of Experimental Social Psychology* 15 (1979):418-34.

[2]David A. Napolitan and George R. Goethals, "The Attribution of Friendliness," *Journal of Experimental Social Psychology* 15 (1979):105-13.

[3]Michael D. Storms, "Videotape and the Attribution Process: Reversing Actors'

and Observers' Points of View," *Journal of Personality and Social Psychology* 27 (1973):165-75.

[4] *New York Times*, 23 November 1982, p. 4.

[5] Cited in Otto Klineberg, *The Human Dimension in International Relationships* (New York: Holt, Rinehart and Winston, 1966), p. 36.

[6] Urie Bronfenbrenner, "Why Do the Russians Plant Trees along the Road?" *Saturday Review*, 5 January 1963, p. 96.

[7] Paraphrased from Murray Bodo, *Francis: The Journey and the Dream* (Cincinnati: St. Anthony Messenger Press, 1979), pp. 16-17.

Chapter 15: Called to Understand

[1] Robert A. Brown, "The Reformed Tradition and Higher Education," *The Christian Scholar* 41 (1958):21-40.

[2] Stanley Milgram, *Obedience to Authority*, pp. 194-97.

[3] John M. Darley and Bibb Latané, "Bystander Intervention in Emergencies: Diffusion of Responsibility," *Journal of Personality and Social Psychology* 8 (1968):377-83.

[4] Arthur F. Holmes, *The Idea of a Christian College* (Grand Rapids, Mich.: Eerdmans, 1975), p. 79.

[5] Malcolm A. Jeeves, *Psychology and Christianity: The View Both Ways* (Downers Grove, Ill.: InterVarsity Press, 1976), p. 85.